The Chameleon Consultant

To those consultants who know that success depends on more than just raw intelligence

The Chameleon Consultant

Culturally intelligent consultancy

ANDREW HOLMES

Routledge
Taylor & Francis Group

LONDON AND NEW YORK

First published 2002 by Gower Publishing

Reissued 2018 by Routledge
2 Park Square, Milton Park, Abingdon, Oxon OX14 4RN
711 Third Avenue, New York, NY 10017, USA

Routledge is an imprint of the Taylor & Francis Group, an informa business

Publisher's Note
The publisher has gone to great lengths to ensure the quality of this reprint but points out that some imperfections in the original copies may be apparent.

Disclaimer
The publisher has made every effort to trace copyright holders and welcomes correspondence from those they have been unable to contact.

Typeset in 9 point Stone Serif by IML Typographers, Birkenhead, Merseyside

A Library of Congress record exists under LC control number: 566084074

ISBN 13: 978-1-138-71823-4 (hbk)
ISBN 13: 978-1-138-71822-7 (pbk)
ISBN 13: 978-1-315-19597-1 (ebk)

Contents

List of tables

List of figures

Preface

I came into consulting comparatively late. Unlike most, who enter straight from university, or after completing their MBA, I spent eight years in industry prior to making the move, so consultancy was a bit of a shock. However, I found it offered opportunities for significant personal development and challenge.

As I moved from sector to sector, organization to organization, I noticed that each client required subtle, and sometimes not so subtle, changes in the way the service was delivered. This suggested that the 'one size fits all' approach was unlikely to work in all circumstances. It also became clear from observing my colleagues that some were more successful at moving between clients and sectors than others. For example, those experienced in one sector, say investment banking, found it very difficult to adjust to a client that fell outside the fast-moving, brash culture that typifies investment banks. The same was true for those working in the public sector who were more familiar with the slow decision-making process associated with government institutions. Such maladjustment often spelt disaster for the consultant who found it difficult to deliver in such an alien environment. And, as we will see later, in extreme cases this can be disastrous for the firm and the client too, with the firm losing fee income (and risking being sued) and the client ending up with a failed project and a bitter experience of using consultants.

Having studied organizational culture as part of my MSc, I began to realize that there was a need to consider this when delivering consultancy services. The need to sensitize consultants as to what to expect *before* they entered the client site for the first time was critical, if only to reduce the shock most consultants experienced when they moved from one client to the next. Equally critical was the need to ensure that the approaches used to deliver the consultancy, such as methods, tools, client management and so on, were also adjusted to fit in with the way in which the client worked. The big question was how this could be done.

Organizational culture is generally inaccessible: it is difficult to describe and can often become too esoteric to be of any use, and people are often switched off by it. Indeed, there are many books on culture, and many models. However, most do not describe culture in a way that provides any basis for the kind of sensitivity I was seeking to generate within my fellow consultants. Then, in between assignments at an investment bank and a United Kingdom government department, I was fortunate enough to spend six weeks at Henley Management College researching this concept. Whilst there, I came across the work of Rob Goffee and Gareth Jones, who had derived what I consider to be an effective model of organizational culture, and one on which it was possible to develop the concept of cultural intelligence. This model described four basic types of culture – networked, mercenary, communal and fragmented – each having its own unique characteristics. More important was the accessibility of the model, and its ability to make the complex nature of culture into something that was easily understood. I believed that if it worked for me it could work for the rest of the consulting community.

The concept of cultural intelligence in consulting is quite simple. If, as a consultant, you are able to adjust your behaviour, approaches and working style to those of the client, you are more likely to succeed, because not only would you be able to reduce the time it takes to adapt to your new client, you would also be able to win their trust more readily. And because the overriding success factor in any consulting engagement is the winning of client trust and commitment, the quicker this is achieved the better the engagement will be for all parties. But all too often the consultant believes he or she can do it by intelligence alone. Outsmarting the client is, unfortunately, not the way to win them over and, if anything, serves to create a bad name for the consulting profession. Lasting value is only achieved by making things happen for a client that can be sustained once you leave. And it is this value that helps to forge long-term client relationships and position the consultant as a trusted advisor.

The Chameleon Consultant will be of interest to consultancy firms and consultants alike. Applicable to the sole trader, the boutique and larger firm, it will prove to be an invaluable reference and guide to improving the entire consulting process, using culture to gain and retain competitive advantage, and deliver client satisfaction.

AH

Acknowledgements

After writing my first book, *Failsafe IS project delivery*, I agreed that I would not write another book for at least a couple of years, if only to spare my family from the endless battle to get me away from my desk. However, after spending time at Henley Management College researching the concept of cultural intelligence, I saw the potential for another. And, in the process of writing this one, I have written two others and have been asked to write two more. Maybe the bug is now too great for me to stop.

As before, I am indebted to a small number of people who provided the necessary support and encouragement along the way. In particular, I would like to thank Professor Gareth Jones with whom I had the privilege to work at Henley Management College. He was able to provide the guidance and challenge that allowed the concept of cultural intelligence to become more than a germ of an idea. I would also like to express my appreciation to HarperCollins, which kindly permitted me to use material from *The character of a corporation* by Rob Goffee and Gareth Jones. In addition, I am grateful to United Feature Syndicate, Inc., which kindly allowed me to use the Dilbert strip that appears at the beginning of Part I. I would also like to thank some additional contributors. First, Cape Consulting, which provided the case study in Chapter 10. This is a company that has truly embraced cultural intelligence. Second, Jacqueline Clarke and Sacha Jensen of Clarke-Wetter, who provided views and opinions on the recruitment, retention and development of culturally intelligent consultants and who added to the quality of the book by linking cultural intelligence to the work of Belbin. Finally, James McColl of the Leverage Group, who provided some perspectives on the qualities of good and bad consultants.

Lastly, I would like to thank my official and unofficial editors. First, Igmar Folkmans, my editor at Gower, who provided some sound ideas on how to enhance the manuscript. And of course my wife, Sally, who once again provided the initial editorial service that ensured the manuscript's quality met her exacting standards.

Introduction

The reasonable consultant adapts himself to the client; the unreasonable one persists in trying to adapt the client to himself.

Have you ever delivered a technically superior performance only to find that your client slated your work and rejected your recommendations? Or maybe you are one of the many consultants that have not hit it off with your clients and either chosen to terminate the assignment or have been asked by your client to leave. If you are among those that have experienced disappointment, this may now be a dim and distant memory. If you have yet to experience failure of any kind within your consulting career, read on and ensure that you are able to maintain your flawless record.

Before continuing, you might want to complete the questionnaire at the start of Part III (p. 127). This will give you an indication of how culturally intelligent your firm already is. And, once you have read the remainder of the book, you should be able to decide on how culturally intelligent you want it to be.

Consultancy is a mix of creativity and discipline, both of which are essential to the delivery of a valued service. One without the other creates an imbalance that leads to a sub-optimum result. The creativity comes from generating solutions to problems and coming up with innovative products and services that are able to address the complex issues faced by organizations. This is important because many companies find it increasingly difficult to navigate through the changes they face whilst maintaining focus on their daily business activities. They just don't have the time to commit to analysing and understanding the problem and its implications for their business. The discipline comes from the ability to cut through the barriers to change by working closely with the client's staff and maintaining the high levels of energy and persistence required to get the job done. Again, many organizations suffer from a general inability to complete change projects, irrespective of whether they are technology- or business-driven. So often other things get in the way, such as politics, or people tire and give up. Excellent consulting also requires a focus on relationship management and a sensitivity to the client's working style. I believe this additional skill necessitates an understanding of, and sensitivity to, the client's culture. Organizational culture exerts a strong force within organizations: it defines how work is executed, how people get on and how they manage change. It also determines how individual functions interact and work together to complete their day-to-day activities, and, on a larger scale, determines the relative success or failure of the organization as a whole. As a consultant who has worked in many different organizations, across many different sectors, I have been surprised at just how different organizations can be, even though many perform similar functions. Much of this difference can be explained by their culture. In essence culture boils down to 'the way we do things around here', which in some organizations is the result of strong leadership, such as that displayed by Jack Welch of General Electric. In others it is created by a combination of market factors, the way managers behave and the norms of behaviour that exist within the groups and functions that make up the organization. Irrespective of how it is created it is this cultural difference between companies that demands that the consultant vary his or her working style in order to deliver the consulting engagement successfully.

In many cases, changes in a consultant's working style tend to result from client push-back and criticism, rather than a deliberate attempt to adapt before the consultant steps onto the client site for the first time. Of course, there are consultants who have learned from the experience, and as a result adapt their style and approach more readily. But because this tends to be intuitive rather than based upon any underlying framework, it can take a long time to develop and can still be a hit-and-miss affair. Accelerating this learning is essential in a competitive climate, particularly as clients have become more sophisticated users of consultancy.

There are, unfortunately, still too many instances where consultants display a singular lack of understanding of organizational culture and, as a result, cause unnecessary turbulence during the engagement (see box containing James McColl's perspectives on good and bad consultants). This, as we shall see later, places the success of the entire engagement at risk, and makes the usually stressful consulting process more stressful for both consultants and clients. It is clear that the ability to adjust working style and delivery approach by organizational culture is a skill that is neither understood nor adopted universally. This is, in part, because of the difficulty in understanding the nuances of organizational culture, and the priority most firms place on technical and delivery skills over the interpersonal skills that are an essential part of consultancy. The argument in this book is that if consultancies and consultants could develop a sensitivity to client culture, it ought to be possible for them to adjust their delivery style quite deliberately to fit within the client's preferred way of working. This would make the transition from client to client a smoother process for the consultant and reduce the levels of stress typically experienced as they move between organizations. It would also create the foundations for successful future engagements and additional fee income. The key to achieving this is to provide a framework of culture that is readily accessible rather than abstract and impractical.

THE GOOD, THE BAD AND THE UGLY – JAMES McCOLL

Consulting companies, big, medium and small, are no more than the sum of the people in them. The mix of people in each firm, its client-sector focus and leadership style create the culture of the firm. There are, however, individuals in each firm that we may consider as good, 'OK' and bad consultants. Those that I consider good are good for a variety of reasons, and I do recognize that this is just my opinion but it has been formed partly out of the 'effectiveness' that the clients perceive. Effectiveness is achieved by having high scores in the following attributes: good listening skills, patient relationship-building skills, enthusiasm and an early instinct for a solution based on experience gained and knowledge learned. Having said that, good consultants are prepared to learn something new every day, and I do not mean that a young consultant is a bad consultant. I just mean that he must not pretend to know something thoroughly about which he knows very little. We all had to learn, and higher education is just a 'stepping-stone', not the end of the learning process.

If asked to describe a bad consultant, the following springs to mind: someone who talks a lot using jargon that makes him sound (he thinks) clever. Good listening skills are vital. If you are going to help the client solve a problem, put yourself in the 'client's shoes'. This can be achieved through building empathy by wanting to learn about the problems, the implication of those problems for the client's customers, people and business, and how that makes him feel. Only then can a consultant become a good consultant. The bad consultant will not 'live' the problem, and therefore will not understand it. The resolution of the problem only comes with true understanding. It is then possible to logically come up with solutions or come up with adaptations of solutions to other, similar, problems.

A bad consultant need not be one that has not worked in the client's business sector. Business problems are business problems, and people are people. A working knowledge of the sector is helpful, but not essential. It does, however, bring an understanding of the language and the conventions. The good consultant admits that he is keen to learn. The bad consultant thinks that he knows it all. That will lead to a poor result, most importantly for the client, secondly the consulting firm and thirdly, the consultant. I believe that there is a natural selection process and clients are not stupid. If a consulting firm does not send the right type of people to its clients, it will, eventually, lose that client and others too, as a consequence. A firm's brand and reputation can be over-traded if standards are not maintained. Clients expect quality, knowledge, objectivity and value for money. Try to fool or patronize the client and the market will, eventually, respond.

The consultancy market

There is no doubt that the appetite for consultancy, no matter what form it takes, is increasing as are the levels of fee income. In the short space of 20 years, the consultancy industry has grown considerably:

- global revenues from management consulting have grown from less than $5 billion to more than $100 billion[1]
- consulting is expected to grow at 16.1 per cent per annum over the next decade;[2] other estimates place this annual growth between 15 and 20 per cent[3]
- the European consultancy market is worth £22.5 billion annually[4]
- the total fee income of the top consulting firms in the United Kingdom increased almost 16 per cent from 1998 to 1999, rising from £3.7 billion to £4.3 billion.[5]

Despite the recent economic slowdown that has spilled over into consultancy and the reduction in headcount that invariably followed, the need for good consultants will continue. And, once economic recovery takes place, there is nothing to suggest that consultancies won't resume the double-digit growth of the past.

The growth of consultancy, and in particular management consultancy, may have been generated by many different factors, but it reflects the increasing complexity and turbulence of the business world, and the need to bring expertise and shared experience to bear on the problems faced by organizations. Typical of such problems is the need to understand the consequences of globalization, how to get the best out of an increasingly disenfranchised workforce, how to address the opportunities and threats posed by e-commerce, how to manage organizational change, how to execute global initiatives and how to manage complex IT implementations. Organizations turn to consultants because of their ability to focus, bring best practice and cut through the politics of change. They also bring them in because they often lack the internal resources, time, expertise or discipline to get the job done. And, of course, there are the odd occasions when they are brought in as scapegoats.

Over the past three years the consulting market has changed. At the top end, the Big Five consultancies (KPMG, Ernst & Young, Accenture/Andersen, PricewaterhouseCoopers, and Deloitte and Touche) are having to revisit their operating models because of the dual pressure of regulatory and technological change. The Securities and Exchange Commission (SEC) in the United States has been concerned for some time at the paper-thin walls that exist between audit and consultancy. The SEC believes that the audit business in each of the Big Five secures work for its management consultancy divisions because of the hold it has over senior executives when auditing their accounts. This is believed to be particularly true in instances where the accounts need to be qualified in some way. Until the recent change in United States administration, the SEC was taking concerted action to force the Big Five to separate their audit and consultancy arms. And, despite the softening of the SEC since the retirement of its president, Arthur Levitt, and the election of a pro-business Republican administration, most of the Big Five have either responded or are in the process of responding to SEC demands. The recent events surrounding the collapse of the United States energy trading company Enron have only served to make the separation of audit and consultancy all the more likely.

In addition to this regulatory pressure, rapid technological change has also encouraged the Big Five to look long and hard at their business models. There are three reasons for this. First, over the last five years many of the Big Five's management consultancy divisions have become solely focused on technology and technological change. As they have concentrated on the delivery of large-scale system implementations the traditional business advisory consultancy has been pushed to the background. Second, the Big Five received a massive shock when the advent of e-commerce led to the emergence of the dotcom start-up craze, which created a huge demand for e-commerce solutions and tempted away a large number of their staff who were seduced by the chance to make their million with share options that went with the job. Despite the failure of many of these dotcom and technology companies, the allure of the technology start-up will remain an issue for the future once stability returns to the technology market and firms recover. And third, because the Big Five are partnerships they lack the access to investment capital that is needed to fund rapid change. In reconsidering their business model the majority felt that their management consultancy divisions had become overly focused on technology and were too investment-hungry to manage. As a result, many firms felt it was time to part company.

The dual pressure of technological change and regulatory intervention has therefore resulted in the majority of the Big Five splitting their management consultancy services divisions from their mainstream auditing activities. For example:

- In May 2000 Ernst & Young sold its management consultancy services arm to Cap Gemini for $11 billion, forming one of the world's largest technology-come-management consultancies.
- In September 2000 PricewaterhouseCoopers (PwC) and Hewlett-Packard were in talks about the possible sale of its management consultancy services division,[6] and within two months the deal was off after the precipitous fall in technology stocks and Hewlett-Packard's reporting poor third-quarter results.[7] The fallout from the collapse of Enron in January 2002 (see next bullet) has resulted in the acceleration of the split of PwC audit and PwC consulting, with PwC Consulting expected to follow an initial public offering route in summer 2002.

- The long-running dispute between Arthur Andersen and Andersen Consulting was resolved during summer 2000. The split has resulted in Andersen Consulting changing its name to Accenture, as it was no longer legally allowed to use the Andersen name. This comes as a blow to Andersen Consulting, which spent $7 billion building up its brand.[8] The name-change alone cost Accenture $100m. Accenture floated on the stock exchange in June 2001, and Arthur Andersen changed its name to Andersen to exploit the brand that was once Andersen Consulting. The future of Andersen is now in doubt following the demise of Enron. This, the largest corporate failure on record, is embroiling the firm in allegations of unprofessional behaviour, including the destruction of audit records after they had been subpoenaed by the SEC. The early indications from press reports suggest that the firm will be subject to multimillion-dollar lawsuits, which may result in the firm's own failure and possible sale. This will have profound impacts on the Big Five, which we are already witnessing. An increasing number of large corporations including the US media group Walt Disney, the British insurer CGNU and the Anglo-Dutch consumer goods company Unilever, will no longer allow their auditors to provide management consultancy services. And as the fallout from the Enron affair continues, further companies are likely to follow suit. All eyes are now on Harvey Pitt, the new chairman of the SEC.
- KPMG floated its American consultancy practice in February 2001 to raise $1.3 billion. The money raised from the float will be used to pay off debt and buy the consulting arms of the KPMG accountancy firm dotted around the globe to form a global consulting organization.[9]

Interestingly, until February 2002 Deloitte and Touche was the only member of the Big Five to refuse to separate its management consultancy and audit divisions. And Stephen Sprinkle, global director of strategy, innovation and eminence, was damning in his criticism of how the others have responded.[10] He viewed the Ernst & Young merger with Cap Gemini as demotivating for the Ernst & Young consultants. He felt they were no longer in a profession but instead were part of a command and control entity that no longer organized itself around projects and results. He believed it had become part of a low-cost body shop. He also felt that those who work for Accenture have lost the career path that existed in the old partnership model. A press release on 6 February 2002, itself in response to the Enron scandal, announced the separation of Deloitte Consulting from the firm.

It is clear that the impact of the dotcom start-up craze has diminished. Indeed, recent analyst reports suggest that organizations wishing to pursue e-commerce should use the Big Five rather than the specialist e-commerce consultancies, many of which have already gone into bankruptcy (not surprising given that the majority had failed to develop a solid business model). Moreover, they believe that the Big Five are in a strong position, having taken the trouble to develop the skills and methods associated with e-commerce. This reflects the talent, skills, infrastructure and resource pools that these firms possess. Until recently the SEC appeared to have relaxed its stance toward audit and consultancy, but the failure of Enron and the indictment of Andersen's in the affair will rekindle the debate about the Big Five. Although it is too early to tell what will happen, it is becoming clear that the SEC will be adopting a much tougher position.

This change in Big Five status is beginning to have an effect on medium-sized consultancies, which are increasingly asked to provide more comprehensive services, especially delivery. As the middle ground opens up, there are likely to be more small- and medium-sized consultancies offering a range of general and specialized services. The consultancy market will therefore see the usual distinction between the larger consultancy firms (providing everything from strategic visioning through to delivery of change via projects and pro-grammes), the boutiques (specialist consultancies offering a narrowly defined service, such as strategy formulation), and the sector specialists (such as those that serve solely the invest-ment banking community, or local government). It will also see a greater number of small- to medium-sized firms offering a range of services across the majority of sectors, albeit at a lower price than that charged by the larger firms. In addition, the technology companies have recognized the need to provide value-added services on top of their product offerings. Many are now reinventing themselves into consultancies. The simple reason for this is that, as the need for hardware diminishes, technology firms need to generate other sources of revenue.

Why cultural intelligence?

Why should consultancies be concerned with the culture of their clients? I believe there are three reasons for this:

1. Consultancies and consultants often assume that they will be 'doing' consulting to the client – that is, believing they (not the client) are in charge, which allows them to run roughshod over the organizations in which they consult. Such an approach requires little consideration of the client's culture, and can lead to consultancy disasters, dissatisfied clients and bruised consultants. It also reduces the likelihood of repeat business. In a world where adding value should be a daily mantra for consultants, this type of approach is increasingly unacceptable.
2. Consultancies fall into the trap of delivering their service in the same way, irrespective of client culture. Such a 'one size fits all' approach to delivery is flawed, as each organization requires a slightly different approach to deliver the service successfully. Clearly method is important, but there is a need to adjust this to client culture. We will see later just how failing to consider the cultural angle can lead to a multimillion-dollar consulting failure.
3. We are in the age of the intelligent customer – organizations are far more experienced in the purchase and use of consultants than they used to be, and now expect greater accountability from the consultants they hire. They also expect more by way of benefits from their consulting investment, which is increasingly in multimillions. Intense economic and competitive pressures are causing organizations to scrutinize all expend-itures, and consultancy spend is no different. With many consultancy assignments falling short of expectations, there is an increasing need to show actual returns from the consult-ing investment.

Increasingly, the success of the consulting engagement depends upon the individual's and firm's ability to work within the client's culture and agenda; that is, to fit in and deliver the engagement according to the grain of the organization. By doing so, they are likely to gain the trust of the client more rapidly, and, as a consequence, deliver the engagement more successfully. However, many consultants and consultancies do not have this skill set, and instead depend upon hard skills, such as technical knowledge, to get the job done. Unfortunately, this cannot guarantee success. And just because an approach is successful in one organization, it does not follow that the results will be the same in another. A consultant who has excellent technical ability, but who adopts an inappropriate stance with the client, is unlikely to generate the trust and working relationship that is so important, especially in the early stages of the engagement. Alternatively, one that has a balanced skill set, which includes a basic understanding of different client cultures, is more likely to succeed.

In recognizing that successful consultancy engagements do not depend on technical skills alone, many of the larger consultancies have been enhancing the consultant's skill set through non-technical training. For example, many have now been trained in the basics of neurolinguistic programming (NLP) and emotional intelligence. This is an important step, because it provides some of the essential coping skills required to succeed in tough assignments. There has also been a lot of interest in working within mixed nationality teams as the need to deliver consultancy engagements for global clients has necessitated working across national borders. Such engagements draw out the significant variations in national culture that exist and that can often present major problems for the consultant. Some of the more enlightened consultancies take the trouble to educate their staff in national cultures. The majority do not, instead relying on the consultant's ability to muddle through. The same is true of organizational culture. And I believe that success in consultancy increasingly depends on developing an understanding of organizational culture and using this to deliver assignments that add real value. From a consultant's perspective it is about using culture as competitive advantage.

Purpose and structure of the book

The purpose of this book is to develop culturally intelligent consultants. In doing so it describes the importance of organizational culture and details how cultural intelligence can be used to enhance each component of the consultancy life cycle. This provides the basis for tailoring consultancy assignments to match client culture. It is not a book that tells you how to set up a consultancy, nor is it about drawing up consultancy contracts, and so on. There are plenty of such books already available. Equally, it is not suggesting a new process for consultancy, as again the model is fairly straightforward, irrespective of the way it is packaged. Instead it is about augmenting what already exists by adding a cultural dimension to it.

The book is structured into three parts. Part I describes the foundations of cultural intelligence. It begins by bringing the reader up to date with the latest thinking on consultancy skills, in particular NLP and emotional intelligence, and widening this to include cultural intelligence. Prior to introducing the model on which cultural intelligence is based, a short departure into organizational culture is necessary to ensure a solid understanding of culture is created. Part II then concentrates on describing how cultural intelligence can be applied across the consultancy life cycle. Each chapter within Part II discusses the implications of cultural intelligence for the key consultancy stage being addressed, and outlines how they can be tailored to meet the needs of the different client cultures represented by the model. Finally, Part III describes what it means to be a culturally intelligent firm, and outlines how consultancies can develop and maintain cultural intelligence by enhancing their recruitment and selection processes, providing basic training and awareness for their consultants, preparing their staff for engagements, updating their tools and techniques, and improving the targeting of their accounts. A bibliography has been included that will provide readers with a wide range of further reading that, together with the concepts described here, will enhance their skills and make them more effective consultants.

The foundations of cultural intelligence

Being a consultant is difficult, but being an effective and successful one is considerably harder.

Although consultancy is one of the most popular professions for graduates, and in particular those with masters degrees in business administration (MBAs), it is extremely tough. Most graduates – be they fresh from business school, or from a period in industry – do not realize just how tough consultancy is until they join. Consultants work long hours, very often away from home, and are always under the spotlight of their clients and paymasters alike. On the one hand, clients expect them to deliver value for the high fees they are charged, no matter what personal sacrifice is required, and on the other, their paymasters expect them to deliver, sell, develop new ideas and products, and share their knowledge whilst delivering high-value client service. Many people new to consultancy have a rose-tinted view of the consultant's lifestyle, and soon find that high salaries require high sacrifice.[1]

DILBERT reprinted by permission of United Feature Syndicate, Inc.

Surviving within the consultancy profession requires many things, not least resilience, high intellect and the ability to get on with a variety of different clients. But one of the key skills that is often missing is the ability to behave and deliver the service in a way that includes the client. To do this successfully requires more than technical skills; it needs a real strength of character and relationship-building and management skills. But even these are not enough, as it also requires an understanding of what works and what doesn't work within the client organization – this is what I term cultural intelligence.

Developing cultural intelligence means understanding organizational culture, but not in a pure academic sense. It means using a practical framework of culture that facilitates the development of a competence that will reduce some of the culture shock experienced by consultants and clients alike as consultants move from one client to another. Part I is therefore designed to develop the foundations on which it is possible to develop the culturally intelligent consultant and consultancy firm. It consists of three chapters:

- Chapter 1 brings the reader up to date with some of the latest thinking about consultancy skills, such as neurolinguistic programming and emotional intelligence, and places these into the wider context of cultural intelligence.
- Chapter 2 discusses the topic of culture, which forms the basis of the cultural intelligence concept. Consultants will come into contact with national, organizational and functional cultures, and each is dealt with. At the end of this chapter the reader will have gained a general understanding of culture in all its guises.

- Chapter 3 introduces the model of culture on which cultural intelligence can be developed, along with an assessment of the dominant behaviours within organizations. Two self-assessment questionnaires have been included within this chapter to allow the consultant to begin to apply the concepts introduced within Part II more readily.

1 *Where does cultural intelligence fit with emotional intelligence and NLP?*

The changing nature of consultancy

For a long time, consultancy was about interviewing clients, writing reports and making recommendations. In such instances it was possible to pull together a small team of consultants and complete the assignment without much need for lengthy client contact. And, because of the limited presence, it was always a hit-and-miss affair whether the organization would implement the advice given. Of course, in those cases where the organization had hired consultants to reinforce and legitimize an internal idea, they were more likely to accept the conclusions, especially if they were the same as those derived internally. It was this sort of assignment that led to the expression 'Give a consultant your watch and they will tell you the time'. However, in response to the increasing scale and complexity of change, and the higher levels of client sophistication, these comfortable days have long since gone. Clients now demand more for their money and are no longer satisfied with fancy reports that gather dust. Instead they want action and usually expect consultants to implement their recommendations.

A recent survey of consultancy highlights some interesting differences between the perceptions of clients and their consultants:[1]

- Whereas over 55 per cent of consultants felt they were good at coming up with original ideas for their clients, only 25 per cent of their clients agreed.
- 40 per cent of clients felt that consultants gave them no new ideas at all.
- It was believed that consultants were good at fleshing out their clients' problems, acting as catalyst for change and delivering results faster than their clients could on their own.
- Value for money was seen to be a real issue. Although this is a particular problem for the Big Five, whose fee rates are typically two to three times that of second and third tier consulting firms, value for money does not wholly relate to fees. It goes much deeper than that. After all, clients will pay more if they believe they are getting the value they expect.
- Over 55 per cent of clients believe that consultants had more loyalty to their firm than them as clients.
- Of the many reasons why clients seek out consultants to help them, the most frequent are:
  - to help them with changing their organization
  - to get them out of a crisis; in essence to supplement their skill requirements where these were lacking
  - to implement change more rapidly than they could themselves

  – facilitate internal processes and to learn from the consultants.

Clients were far less interested in the 'latest thing', be it technology, management techniques or the consultancy's methodology. This suggests that consultancies that pride themselves on fancy methodologies or push the latest buzzwords may be wasting their energy.

The demand for consultancy has grown considerably. As we saw in the Introduction, fee income has risen from $5 billion to over $100 billion in a little under 20 years. This growth has proved to be a double-edged sword for most consultancies. On the one hand profitability has increased sharply, as has the remuneration of consultants and partners alike. Even new graduates without any business or consultancy experience can earn upwards of £30,000 per year. On the other, it has meant that the war for talent, especially within the Big Five consultancies has hotted up. For example, the £600 million increase in fee income for the United Kingdom's top 100 consultancies between 1998 and 1999 is believed to have created between 4500 to 5000 additional consulting posts.[2] And over the last few years, the largest consultancies have introduced significant joining bonuses for new graduates in order to attract them to their firm, rather than a competitor's. In some cases these can be as high as 30 per cent of the first year's salary.

Of course, in the very recent past we have entered a significant downturn and possible recession, itself precipitated by the fallout from the bursting of the technological bubble which started in 2000 and got a whole lot worse in 2001. As this bites, consultancies everywhere are tightening their belts, reducing headcount and freezing recruitment. For example, Accenture has been offering its staff sabbaticals and asking new joiners to defer their start date by up to a year. Most firms have reduced headcount by around 10 per cent. Such adjustments do not reduce the need for reliable, effective and knowledgeable consultants, especially those that are culturally intelligent. If anything it makes it all the more important.

The increasing complexity and global nature of commerce has also had an impact on the consultants themselves. The consultant of today has to endure longer assignments, longer hours and more complex environments, and is under constant pressure to perform. With lengthy assignments, consultants and consultancies alike have had to learn how to work effectively with the client over extended periods. This has led firms to consider skills and attributes that extend beyond those based on intelligence and technical know-how alone. This, of course, is not to say that intelligence is not a factor, as clients still expect to get the best brains for the fees they pay. It merely suggests that client success is not predicated on technical brilliance alone, but on some other skills that are not born out of pure intellectual capability. Consultancies have therefore sought to enhance the skills of their professional staff. Initially focused on relationship management, and client–consultant team working, this has recently been extended into developing skills associated with inter-cultural working, self-awareness, and interpersonal influence.

Consultancy skills

Consultancies work hard to ensure that the people they recruit are able to work to the high standards expected of them. Being an effective consultant is not easy, as there are significant demands placed upon the individual. Nor is survival in the largest consultancies always guaranteed, as, for some, the demands are too great. This is particularly true for those consultants who enter the profession after a significant period in industry. Observation suggests that during the boom times, many firms dropped their guard when it came to recruitment. Because there was such a high demand for consulting staff, people were added to the headcount who were really not suited to the role. Many were not intellectually sharp or inquisitive enough and lacked the core skills of the consultant. As to be expected these were the first to go when the market turned during the second and third quarters of 2001. I believe consultancies need to maintain a high standard across its entire professional staff, which means retaining strict hurdles when recruiting. I will come back to this topic in Chapter 10.

Effective consulting depends on having both breadth and depth in knowledge and experience. This is often referred to as the 'T-shaped consultant', indicating the breadth of knowledge, but also the detailed understanding of specific technologies and sectors. This is important because clients depend on the consultant's ability to bring best practice and other sectorial and organizational experiences to the engagement, as well as the detailed understanding of particular technologies and processes, and working knowledge of the latest management thinking. Table 1.1 highlights the typical skills, attributes and knowledge expected of consultants across three categories:

Table 1.1 Consultancy skills

Client-focused	Firm-focused	Individual-focused
Political sensitivity	Sales	Active listening
Coaching	Marketing	Problem solving
Mentoring	Knowledge management	Analytical thinking
Relationship management	Team working	Conceptual thinking
Team working	Acccount management	Technical knowledge
Project management	Coaching	Industry knowledge
Industry knowledge	Mentoring	Fast thinking
Knowledge transfer	Risk management	Presentation skills
Thought leadership	Project management	Self motivation
Technical knowledge	Strong delivery skills	Adaptability
Programme management	Thought leadership	Persistence
Process expertise	General leadership	Tenacity
Negotiation	Industry knowledge	
	Technical knowledge	
	Programme management	
	Interviewing	

1. Client-focused: such skills are associated with how the consultant delivers the assignment, and as such extends to project management, political sensitivity, as well as the specific technical knowledge brought to the engagement.
2. Consultancy-firm-focused: these are the skills that the consultancy firm expects its professional staff to possess and develop. These number more than those for the client because of the additional need to manage internal work, bring in new business and develop junior staff.
3. Individual-focused: these are the core skills of any consultant, and comprise a mix of knowledge, capability and personal attributes.

The table illustrates the broad range of skills required to be an effective consultant. It also suggests that there a number of core areas.[3]

Looking at Table 1.1 it would be a tall order to find any one consultant with all of the skills highlighted. Collectively, however, consultancies usually possess the majority, if not all, of these skills, and it is this that enables them to field highly effective teams. Also, because the success of an engagement depends on managing more than just technical delivery, skills such as dealing with politics, self-motivation, developing relationships and adaptability are especially important.

Whilst consultancies have always prided themselves on keeping up with the latest management thinking, and translating this into saleable propositions for their clients, until recently it has been rare for them to invest and apply this knowledge internally. However, this has changed over the last few years for a number of reasons:

• The demands placed upon individual consultants have increased substantially. Consultants are expected to absorb vast amounts of knowledge and use this to deliver complex solutions to their clients.
• Consultants are expected to sustain high levels of commitment and motivation, necessary to deliver engagements successfully and progress within the firm.
• There is a desire to maintain a healthy work–life balance. Working very long hours over extended periods is unhealthy, and causes high turnover and burnout rates amongst consultants. With tight employment markets, consultancies cannot afford to lose staff, as they are increasingly difficult and expensive to replace.
• The professional staff of consultancies expect more by way of personal development. No longer satisfied with purely technical training, consultants want to continue to develop their all-round capabilities, which increasingly encompasses self-awareness and self-development.
• The ability to succeed within complex engagements depends heavily on relationship management skills. Such skills are an essential component to the consultant–client dynamic and are key to developing productive long-term client relationships.

This shift to larger-scale engagements, longer-term client relationships, and more complex problems, and the need to maintain an optimum and effective workforce, has forced consultancies to enhance the skills of their professional staff. Such enhancements are not technical, or academic. Instead they are focused on developing self-awareness amongst the staff so that they are aware of how they perform and are enabled to maintain peak performance. These skills are not client-focused, and yet, with them, clients benefit.

The arguments for such self-awareness training are irrefutable. If consultants are able to understand their motivations, values and beliefs, and if they are able to understand how to attain and maintain a peak performing state, they will be less likely to suffer burnout and will be more able to cope with the inevitable setbacks that occur. In addition, if they understand how to influence people more effectively, and manage their own emotions, they will be more capable at bringing the client with them rather than alienating them. Finally, in an employment market where retention is vital, such personal training is well received by the consultants. This is because it is different from the usual kind of technical training they receive and not directly related to a particular product, client or market.

The two key areas in which consultants receive this type of personal training are neurolinguistic programming and emotional intelligence. These are summarized in the following two sections.

Neurolinguistic programming

Research at the University of California in 1972 led to what we now know as neurolinguistic programming (NLP). The research involved modelling three successful therapists in order to establish patterns of successful therapy so that these could be passed on to others. The initial research was further refined and adapted so that it could be used to model patterns of success in any profession. Since then, NLP has taken corporate America by storm with a proliferation of self-help books and motivational seminars based upon its concepts. This is increasingly evident in the United Kingdom.

The neuro (N) component of NLP asserts that our behaviour stems from the way we experience the world around us through our five senses (seeing, hearing, touching, smelling and tasting). It also relates to our physiological reactions to the things we sense. For example, this would include the sensations of excitement, fear and so on when reacting to a specific event. The linguistic (L) element of NLP relates to the language we use to order our thoughts and behaviour, and the way we communicate with those around us. Finally, the programming (P) aspect of NLP refers to the way we, as individuals, choose to respond to the conditions around us. This suggests that we ought to respond in quite deliberate ways to certain situations and stimuli, rather than reacting automatically.

One of the basic tenets of NLP is modelling the success of others: watching how they behave, asking how they became so successful and so on. Taking this notion of modelling to its extreme, NLP is about changing the way we behave in order to become as successful as those we model, and providing those who seek success with the tools with which to do so. And, given that everyone in corporate life wants to be successful, it is no wonder that NLP has become so widely accepted, especially in the United States. It would appear that with NLP anyone can become successful, though of course this is not universally true.

NLP can be broken down into four components:[4]

1. Understanding and changing beliefs. This relates to the way in which individuals believe in their own capabilities and how, by altering their belief system, they can become more effective, and ultimately more successful. Although adjusting one's belief system and patterns of behaviour is not easy, NLP provides some tools with which to do this. These include modelling and visualizing success, re-framing failure as an opportunity to learn, and understanding and adjusting personal values.
2. Maintaining peak motivation and performance. This relates to how individuals develop and maintain peak states by associating these with their physiology. This essentially means identifying physical feelings, body posture and mental images associated with success, achievement and high performance, and replicating these time after time. More importantly, it also means recognizing the physiology associated with low performance and either avoiding it or, having recognized it, switching into a more positive, high-performing state. This plays on the well-known fact that the brain's ability to process information is far greater when a person is in a high-performing state than when they are in a low-performing state or feeling anxious. It also means that, when in a high-performing state, an individual is more resourceful and therefore able to overcome significant obstacles without suffering from setbacks.
3. Developing enhanced communication skills. This is associated with developing a sensitivity for the way in which people communicate – often termed sensory acuity. Of the five senses,

three tend to dominate our communication (seeing, hearing and feeling). And of these, everyone has a preferred sensory style whilst communicating. These are:

- visual: those who prefer to discuss things in a pictorial way and use images and visual forms of language, such as 'I can see that this will work'. Such people tend to be fast talkers and ·pick up concepts very quickly, and may finish other people's sentences. These are the people who will jump to a flip chart or whiteboard at any opportunity.
- auditory: those who prefer sounds tend to use auditory forms of language, such as 'This sounds like a good idea'. They also tend to speak slowly and more carefully. They will tend to be more bookish with a preference for the written word. They will also critique other people's work more readily.
- kinaesthetic: those who are more tactile prefer kinaesthetic language that express feelings and movement, such as 'I would like to kick the idea around for a bit longer, as it doesn't feel right'. Such people tend to be even more careful with their language than those who are dominated by the auditory style. These people tend to be deep thinkers.

Enhancing an individual's communication skills means recognizing the emphasis people place on visual, auditory and kinaesthetic language and mirroring these to develop rapport (see the following point). This extends beyond pure listening skills, and includes assessing people's preferences by observing, amongst others, their eye movement[5] (see Table 1.2).

Table 1.2 Eye movements and communication preferences

Eye position	Communication preference
Up and right, up and left, straight ahead	Visual
Level and left, level and right, down and left	Auditory
Down and right	Kinaesthetic

4. Developing rapport. Rapport is one of the key planks of NLP. In simple terms, it is about being sensitive to the way people behave in terms of body language, eye contact and so on, and matching and mirroring these to generate what is known as rapport (also termed congruence). Rapport creates trust, and once trust has been created it is possible to subtly control another person's behaviour. Such influence should not be underestimated. For example, during the 1984 United States presidential campaign between Ronald Reagan and Walter Mondale, tapes of interviews between the candidates and three news channels, CBS, NBC and ABC, were made as part of an experiment. Excerpts were taken from these tapes in which all references to the candidates were removed. These were then shown, with the sound turned off, to a group of randomly chosen people who were asked to score the expressions of the interviewer concerned. The scoring ranged from 1 (extremely negative) to 21 (extremely positive). Whereas two of the interviewers were scored much the same for each candidate (Reagan and Mondale), the ABC interviewer was rated much higher when talking to Reagan. The researchers concluded that this represented a significant bias toward Reagan. This initial finding was followed up to see what the impacts were on the voters themselves. The results were profound. In every case where voters had watched the ABC interview, they voted for Reagan in greater numbers than those who had watched either CBS or NBC. It appeared that the facial expressions used by

the ABC presenter were enough to influence the electorate to vote for Reagan rather than Mondale.[6] This experiment was repeated in subsequent presidential campaigns with similar results.

Each of these four components can be built up into a model that frames how the outcomes we seek can be achieved (Figure 1.1).[7] Each element of the NLP model is part of a complete system. The internal aspects of thinking and feeling affect our external behaviours, which in turn affect the outcome achieved. There are two key points about this model. The first is that the context of the environment or situation we are in will affect the relative importance and interaction between each of these components, and this will affect the outcome of the event we are reacting to. The second point is that the left-hand components of the model exert a much stronger influence over our behaviour than those on the right. This is because beliefs and values are generally much harder to change than our outward behaviours.

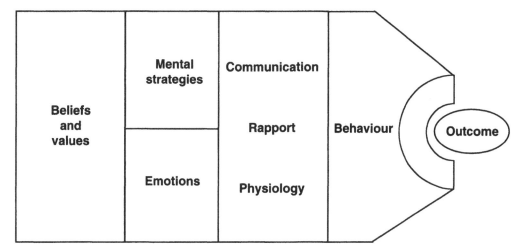

Figure 1.1   The NLP model

Emotional intelligence

Unlike NLP, emotional intelligence is a comparatively new concept, having gained popularity through the publication of Daniel Goleman's book *Emotional intelligence*[8] in 1996.

The roots of emotional intelligence lie in research at New York University that discovered the significant role of the amygdala in controlling our emotions.[9] The amygdala is part of the brain's emotional system, known as the limbic system, and can be considered to be a database of emotional memories. These memories are crude, pre-programmed responses to external stimuli. For example, if confronted by a tiger, the amygdala would cause the person confronted to run; there would be little value in taking time to weigh up options or to consider the outcomes in more detail. The reason for this is that information reaches the amygdala before those parts of the brain that are responsible for reasoning. This means that an emotional response to a situation can override the more rational response derived from the cortex, which processes a much wider set of information, itself necessary to develop a considered response. Emotional intelligence therefore depends on our ability to understand

and control our automatic responses created by the amygdala, and reversing the tendency for emotions to override reasoning.

From a working perspective, being able to control our emotions is important because being successful is not predicated on academic intelligence alone. Research has shown that the smartest people, who seemingly have little control over their emotional life, fare much worse in their careers and personal lives than those who have a balance between academic and emotional intelligence. Indeed, it is usual to find an intellectually gifted person working for a less intelligent, but much more socially adept and rounded individual.

Emotional intelligence falls into five broad areas:[10]

- Being self-aware. This relates to being able to accurately assess how we feel emotionally and what this means to how we behave; understanding our limitations, strengths and weaknesses, and being self-assured.
- Managing the effects of our emotions. This means using our emotions quite deliberately rather than reacting automatically to events. The ability to manage our emotions extends to keeping negative emotions in check, being able to rebound after a setback, being adaptable in times of change and maintaining standards of integrity.
- Maintaining motivation. This relates to the ability to maintain motivation under a variety of different circumstances, and includes the ability to self-motivate, persist without giving in, delay gratification and so on. It has been found that people with this ability tend to be the most productive and effective in all of their undertakings. They also tend to be more successful.
- Understanding the emotions of others. This means paying attention to how other people feel and being attuned to the subtle signals displayed by others as you interact with them. It also extends into political astuteness and interpreting the power-based relationships that exist within organizations.
- Managing relationships. This covers how relationships in their widest sense are managed effectively. As expected, this includes how people are influenced, how they communicate, how relationships are developed and nurtured, and how teams are managed to achieve their goals.

The need to be emotionally intelligent is more important than ever, as people need these types of skills and capabilities to cope with the increasing pace of change. In particular, it is the implications of technological change, globalization and downsizing that require such increased levels of emotional intelligence. Each has exposed people to greater challenges, more complexity and greater stresses. Moreover, because being successful in these turbulent times increasingly depends upon how well people work together, being emotionally intelligent is vital if the dynamics of a team are to generate successful outcomes. Without the ability to control our emotions, motivation and behaviour, it is very difficult to succeed in any undertaking. This is especially true of consultancy.

From the foregoing summaries of NLP and emotional intelligence it should be obvious just how much they overlap. Both focus on how we as individuals manage our personal states and emotions, maintain our motivation, and deal with other people and survive under a variety of different circumstances. Collectively they provide the basis of self-management.

Where does cultural intelligence fit?

So far we have discussed how consultancies are developing their staff to have a much better understanding and application of the softer side of consulting rather than focusing on just academic brilliance. This presents clear advantages to those consultancies who employ such people, not least those associated with having consultants who are well balanced, are able to cope with complex and stressful engagements, and have the influencing skills to engage and win the trust of their clients.

Because it is crucial to balance being smart with being able to manage oneself and the client, it is the combination of all three intelligences that creates the basis for effective consulting; focus on any one to the detriment of the others and there is a strong chance that the engagement or client relationship will be sub-optimal. For example, relying on just intelligence (IQ) may provide great solutions to problems, but there is the very real danger that these may be impossible for the client to implement or sustain once the consultants have left. Moreover, consultants who major on IQ alone tend to be useful only where highly specialized knowledge is required, and more often than not are allowed to beaver away with only minimal client contact. Such focus is, of course extremely important, but client involvement is equally vital. Unfortunately, super-smart people may lack some of the essential human sensitivities that are important within the client–consultant relationship. Those consultants that focus on purely NLP to the detriment of IQ and emotional intelligence often want everyone to achieve everything and become successful. This is often done without any regard to organizational politics and, depending on the client, can be construed as being over the top, or too unfocused to deliver. Finally, controlling emotions without taking into account the rapport building elements of NLP can result in the consultant's becoming a control freak: cold, unemotional, and an automaton.

What is required is a balance between all three. Bringing all three 'intelligences' together creates the basis for a balanced consultant who can apply their intellect, personal motivational skills and emotions to whatever situation they find themselves in. And on this basis the consultant is likely to be more successful than those that don't have such balance. This implies that consultancy firms should broaden the training and development of their professional staff so as to develop a workforce that is not only intelligent from an academic sense, but also from an emotional and personal motivational sense.

Balancing the hard-edged intelligence with the more subtle aspects of emotional control, personal motivation and client influence is necessary if the consultant is to be able to adjust to each new assignment. However, this model as it stands misses one important component: context.

UNDERSTANDING CONTEXT

Context is an extremely powerful determinant of success in consultancy because it dictates the nature and requirements of the engagement. The context of each engagement is normally determined by a small number of components, including:

- the strategic intent of the organization
- the scale of the change the organization is trying to achieve
- the level of technological dependence, which determines the sophistication and complexity of any technological solution

- the nature of the client's competitive position
- the speed at which change must be implemented
- the size, composition and geographical spread of the organization
- the industry sector, or sectors within which the organization operates
- the general state of the national and global economies.

These factors set the technical context for engagement. That is, what the solution will look like, what tasks have to be executed to implement the solution, and how many consultants will be required to deliver it. Consultancies consider these technical aspects very well by focusing on the operating context of the client, what its specific problems are and by considering the wider internal and external environments that are causing the client to undertake major change. This type of technical context setting is something that is deeply embedded within consultancies and can be seen in the way they capture, share and exploit their human and intellectual capital. And it can be argued that this type of technical understanding fits neatly within the IQ component of the consultant's skill set because it depends on solving the problems faced by clients using a combination of knowledge, expertise and best practice.

However, there is another dimension to context that falls outside of the technicalities of a solution. Context is also created by the organization itself by the way it goes about its daily business. It is the culture (or 'the way we do things around here') that creates this context, as it defines how work is executed, how people progress within the company, how people work together, and how the power and political landscapes affect the collective activity of the organization. It therefore follows that understanding this additional dimension to the engagement's context would allow the consultancy (and consultant) to adjust the way in which the technical solution is delivered. Indeed, depending on the nature of the client's culture, it may even affect the solution itself.

Enhancing our understanding by placing the three components of IQ, NLP and emotional intelligence within the wider context of an organization's culture should enhance the consultancy proposition. This implies that it ought to be possible to adjust the way in which the hard (IQ) and soft (NLP and emotional intelligence) consultancy skills are applied within the engagement by understanding how the client works. That is by having cultural intelligence.

There are two aspects worth emphasizing:

1. IQ, emotional intelligence and NLP are predominantly consultant-focused, as each describes attributes of consultant effectiveness. When applied correctly they provide the foundation of engagement success by furnishing the consultant with the techniques and tools they need to succeed in the delivery of the engagement's technical tasks. Although mainly focused on the consultant, there is also a softer dimension to these attributes that includes relationship management, rapport-building and enhanced communication skills.
2. Cultural intelligence is principally client-focused because it is designed to address that part of context that is determined by the way the client carries out its day-to-day activities. This aspect of context is created by a combination of things that make up an organization, including rules and policies; goals and measures; rewards and recognition; staffing and selection; training and development; ceremonies and events; leadership; communications; the physical environment, organization and structure; and market segment.[11] It follows therefore that, as well as using the technical context to frame the

engagement, the cultural dimension can be used by the consultant to adjust the way in which the engagement is delivered. Understanding the cultural dimension ensures the consultant is able to tailor their other skills (IQ, emotional intelligence and NLP) to suit the client culture. Observation alone tells us that working in a culture that is performance-oriented and informal in nature, and which prefers fast-paced change, would require a very different approach to the engagement than one that is conservative and formal in nature, and prefers a more sedate pace of change. Knowing this before the sale is made, and the engagement executed, allows the consultant (whether selling or delivering) to adjust more readily to the client context. This should lead to a more successful outcome for all concerned (consultant, client and consultancy firm).

Benefits of emotional intelligence, NLP and cultural intelligence

Shifting the consultant away from the purely intelligence-driven form of delivery to one that creates a balance between the soft and hard consulting skills is essential if consultancies are to continue to deliver high-value services to their clients. I believe that it is the combination of emotional intelligence, IQ, NLP and cultural intelligence that forms the basis of this balance. It is clear that each of the four components has its own advantages (Table 1.3), but their true value is created when they are brought together. It is this combination of skills that separates the mediocre consultant from the high performers.

Table 1.3   Advantages of the four consultant intelligences

Emotional intelligence	IQ	NLP	Cultural intelligence
• Ensures consultants recognize and understand the implications of different emotional states for their outward behaviour • Provides the basis for managing emotional states under specific contexts • Allows consultants to develop a sensitivity to other people's emotional states • Allows consultants to manage their motivation, particularly when faced with a challenging situation	• Forms the basis for strong analytical and problem-solving skills • Ensures the development of rapid thinking skills • Provides the basis for fast knowledge transfer and assimilation	• Allows consultants to determine their peak performing state and use this to maintain high performance • Provides the basis for rapid rapport-building with clients • Allows consultants to understand the behaviour of others • Provides the tools and techniques through which consultants can influence clients on a one-to-one basis • Provides consultants with a framework for self-analysis and the basis for adjusting their behaviour	• Allows consultants to develop a sensitivity toward organizational culture • Provides the basis of tailoring the engagement to suit client culture • Allows consultants to pre-sensitize themselves to the types of behaviour expected of them prior to going on site • Ensures the focus of any sales presentation is pitched so that it meets the cultural emphasis of the client • Provides the basis for developing relationship-management strategies suited to different client cultures

The mix provided across the four 'consultancy intelligences' is capable of serving the consultant extremely well, for example:

- At the time of the sale, the consultant is able to assess the client culture and from this determine how the proposition should be presented. Couple this with presenting the correct technical details and using some of the concepts of NLP, and the sale should be more successful.
- Before the engagement, consultants can be pre-sensitized to the client culture and hence know what to expect once on site. This ensures that the consultants behave and work in a way that is acceptable to the client from day one, and as a result are more likely to develop client trust more rapidly.
- During the engagement, the consultants will blend in more effectively with client staff by working in a way that is culturally acceptable. Again, combining this ability with the advantages provided by NLP, emotional intelligence and the raw intelligence of IQ provides the foundation for a successful engagement.

Summary

In this chapter, I have discussed the changing nature of consultancy, now a long way away from the comfortable days of just writing reports. The change in client expectation, itself the result of the rapidly changing business environment, has led to more demanding consultancy assignments. At the same time, there has been unprecedented growth in consultancy as more organizations turn to consultancies to help solve their increasingly complex problems. These changing demands have called for a better, more comprehensively skilled consultant who is able to bring more than just their raw intelligence to the job in hand. Increasingly important are the skills associated with personal motivation, rapport-building and managing long-term client relationships. Consultancies have started to train their consultants in self-awareness techniques, such as NLP and emotional intelligence, in order to improve their staff retention as well as their performance whilst on site. However, although these new skills have helped consultants to cope with longer assignments, and manage the client–consultant relationship more effectively, they need to become more skilled at understanding and adjusting to the context of the client, in essence their culture. This will, along with the other intelligences of IQ, NLP and emotional intelligence, allow the creation of a high-performing, culturally sensitive consultant. In the next chapter, we will review what we currently know about culture.

2 Understanding organizational culture – underpinning cultural intelligence

A culture has the power and authority not only to determine lifestyle but also to form individual personality traits, behaviours and attitudes.[1]

Culture has become a powerful way to hold a company together against a tidal wave of pressures for disintegration, such as decentralisation, downsizing, and de-layering. At the same time the traditional mechanisms for integration – hierarchies and control systems, among other devices – are proving costly and ineffective. Culture is what remains to bolster a company's identity and without it a company lacks value, direction and purpose.[2]

Before we can introduce the model on which the cultural intelligence concept is based, it is necessary to spend some time covering its cornerstone: organizational culture. We should not underestimate the power culture has over the day-to-day operation of a business, how it evolves, how it competes and how it attracts and retains its talent. From a consultant's perspective it is the culture of the organization that is of primary interest because it is at the organizational level where the interaction between consultant and client takes place.

According to Schein, who has written a considerable amount about culture and its relevance to organizations, culture resides at three distinct levels, with each representing a deeper understanding of its nature:[3]

1. Artefacts: this is the most superficial level of culture. It is what you physically see, hear and experience around you as you go about your daily activities. Noticing how people interact, the number of meetings, how noisy or quiet the office is and so on will provide a superficial indication of culture. What you don't understand at this level is why people you observe behave the way they do.
2. Espoused values: these describe a deeper level of culture through such things as organizational strategies, goals, rules and procedures. They essentially justify why people behave they way they do. Espoused values are also reflected in what people say and do when conducting their daily activities. Such things as 'teamwork is really important around here' or 'we like to focus on the job, rather than talking and socializing at work' all help to describe culture. But this is still at a level that does not make it easy to distinguish one organization's culture from another.
3. Shared tacit assumptions: these are the unwritten rules of culture, the things that are taken for granted but remain hidden from view. It is at this level where people are bought into the culture, and it is here where people can fail if they don't fit in. Organizations that have grown up from small beginnings, such as Microsoft and Hewlett-Packard, have

cultures that have endured over time. When these companies were established the entrepreneurs agreed some general rules of engagement about how they would operate, which after time became unwritten and accepted as 'the way we do things around here'. New employees will have been recruited in that image, and so, over time, a consistent culture will have been developed and maintained. For example, the 'HP way' is still deeply embedded within Hewlett-Packard even now.

For the purpose of this book we are interested in understanding culture at a level which allows a consultant to interpret it and adjust to it. So, taking Schein's typology, we need to get to the shared tacit assumptions as soon as possible. We are less concerned about the process through which cultures are changed either by the consultant or the senior executives within an organization. This is a complex undertaking, and consultancies usually undertake this kind of assignment as part of a wider change management engagement. Moreover, there are plenty of well-trodden processes available that can guide the consultant through this type of activity. What follows therefore is a review of culture that forms the backdrop to the model introduced within the next chapter.

What we know about organizational culture

Although the term culture had its origins within anthropology, interest in organizational culture started to gain popularity within business circles only during the late 1970s and early 1980s, when the management theorists of the day, such as Charles Handy, started to discuss the workings of organizations in terms of their culture. But it was the publication of *In search of excellence* by Peters and Waterman in 1982[4] that ensured culture entered the mainstream of business thinking. The authors linked the strength of an organization's performance to its underlying culture, and asserted that successful organizations shared certain common cultural characteristics. And, even though many of the organizations considered excellent when the book was published subsequently lost their lustre – of the 43 excellent companies identified in 1982, only 33 per cent remained excellent five years later[5] – interest in culture remained. For example, other books followed that described the major benefits of strong cultures, as well as the importance of strong leadership in creating and maintaining an organization's culture. As expected, organizations themselves latched onto this interest, and, within a short space of time, culture had gained a special place in the language of management.

Culture is often boiled down to the 'way we do things around here'. And the 'way we do things around here' is usually considered to encapsulate a number of things, including the shared assumptions, behaviours and habits of those employed by the organization, together with the symbols and language used to reinforce the organization's core values. This shared meaning is typically expressed both formally through the rules, structure, hierarchy, pay and reward mechanisms of the organization and informally through the way teams function and the way individuals are treated by their peers. As we noted in Chapter 1, culture is also believed to be created and reinforced through the primary processes of the organization, including: rules and policies; goals and measures; rewards and recognition; staffing and selection; training and development; ceremonies and events; leadership and behaviour; communications; the physical environment and organizational structure.[6] As the processes connected with these ten areas are brought into contact during each working day, they collectively make up the environment that surrounds the workforce. This organizational environment in turn creates and reinforces the organization's culture. Process is of course not the only thing that forms and perpetuates culture, as the desire to conform and be part of a cohesive group is a strong influence on developing habitual behaviours and predictability within individuals. Moreover, predictability is believed to be the mainstay of organizational and individual performance, and it is this that creates the common behaviours that can be called culture.[7] It follows therefore that those who act in an unpredictable way in relation to the prevailing norms of behaviour will not survive for long, as the following examples from Charles Schwab, the online investor, and Standard Chartered illustrate.[8]

> Culture is a de facto recruiting, staffing and procedures tool, naturally winnowing out people and behaviours that don't support our values and our mission. Since we have a very clear set of values to guide behaviour, and since people believe in those values, the chances are pretty high that they'll do the right thing in any situation . . . Just as culture guides those who are in alignment, it opens the exit door for those people who don't share the values. For example, Schwab is team oriented and rejects self-servers very quickly.

> Standard Chartered's old colonial culture simply couldn't cope with a new style banking chief, as is borne out by the departure of Rana Talwar, the bank's charismatic chief executive. He was hired three years ago from Citigroup, the US financial services group, to challenge the traditional way in which StanChart conducted business . . . But his modern management style appears to have proved too much for Sir Patrick Gillam, StanChart's chairman, to cope with. He is the second chief executive to have fallen out with Sir Patrick in three years . . . Patrick did not like the pace of change which Rana was driving. Standard is an old-fashioned, Anglo-Saxon institution.

Describing an organization's culture can go well beyond the basic tenets of the way people behave. Such extensions to the cultural debate can be useful, although they are often quite inaccessible to the casual observer. For example, some believe it is possible to read the mind of the organization by somehow getting into its psyche, whilst others believe an organization exhibits a kind of personality similar to individuals. The latter can be a useful indicator to the consultant, however, as it suggests how the organization views itself, how it wishes to be perceived by its customers, and what it expects of its employees. For example, McDonald's believes itself to be friendly, fun-loving, and dependable; Nike athletic, outdoors, self-improvement-focused, determined and ambitious; whilst 3M sees itself as an innovator.[9]

It is also clear from the literature that there is a strong link between an organization's culture and its performance. Strong cultures are capable of increasing revenues and stock market performance far beyond those that are felt to have unhealthy or weak cultures. In addition, they are more likely to attract talent in greater numbers which in turn allows the organization to increase its market value, perception and ultimately its profits. Thus culture has the ability to create virtuous circles if strong, and vicious circles if weak. This, of course, cannot be accepted as being universally true in all circumstances, because organizations with strong cultures can find themselves in difficulty. We saw this with IBM in the early 1990s when it had to fundamentally shift its culture to prevent its imminent failure when the computing market embraced personal computers. IBM had grown arrogant on the self-belief that no one could threaten its market position.

If we accept the basic determinants of culture as a given and that it is important to organizations, we can introduce a simple and effective model of culture on which we can develop the concept of cultural intelligence for the consulting community. Before doing this we need to complete our review of culture by looking at why organizations remain interested in culture, and briefly describe its national and functional dimensions.

Why organizations are interested in culture

Since organizational culture entered the mainstream of business thinking, consultants, business leaders and academics have maintained their interest in it for a variety of reasons. In particular, three have been especially significant over the past couple of decades:

- the implications of globalization
- the effects of downsizing on organizational performance
- the difficulties experienced in merging and acquiring companies.

THE IMPLICATIONS OF GLOBALIZATION

In a 1983 *Harvard Business Review* article Theodore Levitt[10] argued that technology was creating global markets on a previously unimagined scale of magnitude. This he believed would result in major corporations and brands taking over the global marketplace, driving out both regional and local companies and differences. According to Levitt, multinationals would rule the roost. Indeed, there can be no question that the world is shrinking, as even as far back as 1990 the total of all measured goods and services sold internationally was $4.5 trillion, suggesting that information, products, services, capital and labour were moving freely across international borders.[11]

It was during the 1970s that a number of factors came together that moulded globalization into what we know today. These were:[12]

- the internationalizing of capital markets; the flow of capital across the world is now a 24-hours-a-day phenomenon
- the expansion of international securities investment and bank lending, which has allowed companies and countries to fund their growth
- the increasing sophistication of information technology used within commerce, especially communication via satellite and fibre optic cables; companies can literally work on a continuous basis effectively passing activity from one time zone to another
- the emergence of the Internet: despite the bursting of the electronic commerce bubble of 2000 and 2001, the Internet is a significant business tool that allows businesses to advertise and sell their products
- the economic competition from Japan: since the late 1990s the significance of the Japanese economy and its competition has reduced, primarily through economic stagnation
- the General Agreement on Tariffs and Trade (now succeeded by the World Trade Organization) which heralded the beginnings of a truly global economy through the reduction of destructive protective government policies (taxes for imports and subsidies for locally produced goods and services) that prevented the flow of trade across the world
- the reduction in state control and the subsequent rise in deregulation: this has had a huge

impact on the way transnational corporations have been able to dominate the global economy – many are now more economically powerful than whole nations, giving them significant political muscle in respect of taxation, location and subsidies, whilst individual nations are increasingly offering attractive incentives to such organizations to locate their factories in their country rather than elsewhere
- the oil crisis which brought into sharp relief the dependence on fossil fuels and the need to protect local and global economies against shock events.

The impact of globalization on the flow of capital and the growth of world trade has been enormous. For example, annual average percentage growth of world trade rose from 4 per cent between 1853 and 1913, to 6 per cent between 1950 and 1985, and 7.5 per cent between 1985 and 1996. At the same time trade between companies has risen from 10 to 40 per cent.[13]

Although global domination by a few companies has yet to occur, globalization has forced organizations to deal with much higher levels of competition than they have been previously used to. The days of captive markets are well and truly over; barriers to entry have lowered considerably through competitive legislation; margins have been squeezed through the availability of cheaper labour across the globe; and the ability of customers to take their business elsewhere has increased sharply. This is particularly the case with electronic commerce. As well as the general financial implications of globalization, organizations have had to deal with a number of cultural implications, including:

- maintaining a consistent brand
- conducting business with a wider variety of nationalities, requiring them to take into account variations in business etiquette
- maintaining consistency in corporate culture, policy and standards across different operating regions
- working within multicultural teams.

Being an effective global company requires a much deeper understanding of the variations between national cultures and how these affect the day-to-day operation of the company. Not surprisingly, many multinationals have taken the trouble to identify and nurture global citizens amongst their ranks who are capable of working across different national cultures whilst still retaining the underlying organizational culture. The Swedish corporation ABB typifies the type of consistency any organization that trades globally aspires to. Since its creation through the merger of ASEA of Sweden and Brown, Boveri & Cie of Switzerland, it has achieved an amazing degree of convergence and consistency across a wide range of countries and cultures, as the following illustrates:

> The story is told that a group of ABB managers were gathered from throughout the world for a seminar. None had met before. Yet, they all presented astonishingly similar pictures of the corporation. In other companies, managers would still be arguing at the end of the week. At ABB there is unparalleled consensus of purpose and culture. And this is despite the fact that ABB expects its local companies to operate very much as local concerns. Despite the complexity, the organization manages to send and echo clear and consistent messages.[14]

THE EFFECTS OF DOWNSIZING

The drivers that led to downsizing were principally associated with the globalization of commerce and the impacts of technological change. The fiercely competitive global economy led many organizations – particularly in the United States and the United Kingdom – to cut costs in response to the availability of cheap labour elsewhere, particularly in the Far East, China and India. And, given that the principal cost for any organization is its labour, it was this that bore the brunt. For example, between 1980 and 1993 Forbes 500 companies shed 8 million employees.[15] And, despite the usually positive impacts on the bottom line such headcount reductions had in the short-term, many organizations came to lament the time when they cut headcount with such gusto. For those that made deep cuts there has been a realization that downsizing has broken the psychological contract between themselves and their employees. As a result, organizations can no longer depend on their staff being more committed to the organization than themselves. For many, this has led to poorer financial performance, plus a general lack of loyalty to the firm. Moreover, there is plenty of evidence from corporate America that downsizing has worsened company performance rather than enhanced it. For example, in one study of 531 large corporations, more than three-quarters had cut their payrolls. Of these:

- 55 per cent sought higher profits, but only 46 per cent of these achieved any increase at all
- 58 per cent sought higher productivity, but only 34 per cent of these managed even a small increase
- 61 per cent wanted to improve customer service, but only 31 per cent of these actually did
- within one year following the cuts more than a half had refilled the axed positions.[16]

It is also believed that downsizing has destroyed much of the cultural glue that held organizations together. It is ironic that many are now trying to re-establish what has been destroyed.[17] Downsizing has resulted in the contract between employer and employee becoming too one-sided. For example, instead of being balanced, with the employer offering security in exchange for commitment and responsiveness, it has become weighted towards the employer, who still expects commitment and flexibility, but offers only insecurity in return.[18] Furthermore, in times of tight employment markets, particularly within professional service firms (which bore the brunt of the headcount reductions during the 1990s), staff are more likely to change jobs than remain with their current employer. What is more worrying is that such one-sidedness means that employees are generally less committed to their employer and are no longer willing to go the extra mile. This can have a significant impact on the bottom line because employees turn up for work, switch off and do the bare minimum to get the job done. This is not unique to Anglo-Saxon companies, as similar problems are now appearing in the Far East, especially Japan, where companies had for a long time looked after their employees practically from the cradle to the grave. With an almost bankrupt economy, Japanese organizations can no longer offer the security that they once did, and are having to face up to the harsh realities of the market and global economies.

Recreating an organization's cultural glue once destroyed is not easy, but the rewards can be great because reducing staff turnover can have major impacts on an organization's profitability. For example, one company managed to halve its staff turnover and improve its profitability by around £22 million[19] – a compelling argument for creating a working environment that is capable of meeting employee needs as well as those of the employer.

A final problem with downsizing is that it reduces staff confidence. It is well known that those people who are concerned about their job tenure tend to be less productive than those who are not. This is because they believe they have lost control over their working life, have lost faith in their managers and worry about their ability to get another job if they lose their current one.[20]

MERGERS AND ACQUISITIONS

Driven by globalization, surging stock markets, and economic or strategic barriers to organic growth, mergers and acquisitions have become the primary means by which organizations can grow revenues.[21] However, mergers and acquisitions usually bring with them significant headaches when it comes to the integration of the two organizations. This includes bringing together two sets of information systems, pay and grading systems, reporting structures, processes and particularly cultures. Surprisingly, this is equally the case for those organizations that exist within the same market sector. Although outwardly they may appear the same, once deep into the detail, problems can arise, especially related to who holds the power and whose is the dominant culture. One therefore has to doubt the efficacy of mergers and acquisitions, as the majority of the pain occurs after the deal (the easy part) has been done, and the benefits, so carefully identified at the time of the merger, fail to materialize. The following statistics suggest just how difficult this can be:[22]

- just 23 per cent of all acquisitions earn their cost of capital
- in acquired companies, 47 per cent of executives leave within the first year and 75 per cent within the first three years
- synergies projected for M&A deals are not achieved in 70 per cent of cases
- in the first four to eight months that follow a deal, productivity may be reduced by up to 50 per cent
- a survey of the top 700 cross-border deals in 1998–99 involving 107 companies showed that 83 per cent had added no value after 12 months
- an American study of nine bank mergers showed that, whilst they all led to cost cutting, only four improved efficiency.

It has also been shown that many mergers fail because of the lack of cultural synergy between the merging organizations. It is ironic that chief executives, so keen to seal the deal and promote the similarities and synergies of the two merging companies, often cite people and cultural problems as the primary reason for merger failure. It is equally ironic that the majority of the cultural problems that arise during a merger or acquisition usually emanate at board level.

As we have seen, mergers and acquisitions are increasingly prevalent within professional service firms and consultancies. And, just like other mergers, these are not without their cultural problems. In some respects these can be worse. For example, the $11 billion purchase of Ernst & Young's management consultancy services division by Cap Gemini in May 2000 raised some difficult issues, as the following three quotes, from an article that appeared in *Forbes Global* magazine nine months after the merger, suggests:[23]

As partners in a private firm, the E&Y consultants had grown comfortable running their business on lousy, or non-existent, forecasting and with a pay system that rarely penalized poor performers. Unwin has shaken them up, imposing tough review standards, firing 25 of the original 508 partners and instituting a new pay plan. It has been a rocky nine months. The attrition rate hit a peak of 27 per cent, and morale of the pampered partners plummeted.

The firm's internal problems are hardly over. To some, the upheaval has come with a price – the loss of the collegiality that's found at many partnerships. 'Ernst & Young gave up its cultural dimension for pursuit of capital.'

Titles matter. E&Y managers proud to have been made partners became mere vice presidents. Many soon-to-be partners equally alienated, quit. Other consultants said that the number-crunching created a less personal atmosphere, breaking down the inherent trust among many partners.

Other examples include:[24]

- retail merger failed after ten months when the differences in management style between the two CEOs could not be reconciled; this was after repeated attempts at cultural integration failed
- two financial services organizations concluded that their fundamental cultural differences surrounding perks, incentives and leadership style would mean that they could never fully integrate.

These types of cultural and integration issues can be very significant, and they must be overcome as fast as possible if the newly merged organization is to be successful. The longer the infighting and rivalries persist between the merging organizations, the greater the damage to the bottom line, as executives remain more concerned with their position and status within the new organization than the needs of their customers.

By illustrating the types of cultural issues facing organizations today, we can see that culture remains an important factor in creating a cohesive and successful organization. Therefore, understanding culture in its fullest sense is an important quality for those wishing to navigate their way around an organization whether they are part of it, or are wishing to consult within it.

The wider cultural context – national and functional cultures

It should be recognized that an organization's culture does not exist in isolation, as there are two other dimensions that must be considered. These are the national and functional dimensions. Ultimately, however, national, organizational and functional cultures are interlinked, and all, in one way or another, affect the way we as individuals behave (Figure 2.1).

Although for the purposes of the consultancy engagement it is the overall organizational culture that the consultant should be interested in, it is highly likely that the consultant will have to consider these other dimensions at some stage or another. In particular, when working on a global assignment, the consultant will come across some of the subtle, and not so subtle, variations that exist between different nationalities. And, when working on cross-functional projects, they will almost certainly have to deal with functional cultures. The next two sections describe what we know about national and functional cultures.

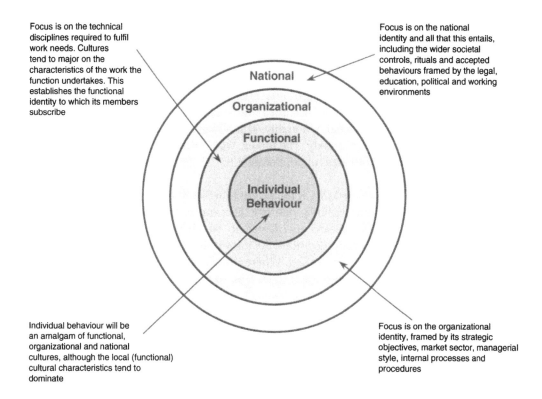

Focus is on the technical disciplines required to fulfil work needs. Cultures tend to major on the characteristics of the work the function undertakes. This establishes the functional identity to which its members subscribe

Focus is on the national identity and all that this entails, including the wider societal controls, rituals and accepted behaviours framed by the legal, education, political and working environments

National

Organizational

Functional

Individual Behaviour

Individual behaviour will be an amalgam of functional, organizational and national cultures, although the local (functional) cultural characteristics tend to dominate

Focus is on the organizational identity, framed by its strategic objectives, market sector, managerial style, internal processes and procedures

Figure 2.1   The hierarchy of culture

NATIONAL CULTURES

National cultures are clearly important to any consultancy that sells its services to multinational clients. It is also vital for anyone working in a global organization, or one in which working within multicultural teams is expected. To address the increasing significance of globalization, most of the major consultancies have established footholds within the principal nations that buy their services. For example, it is now believed that the world's top 40 consultancies generate anywhere from half to three-quarters of their revenues outside the United States. Accenture has over 4000 consultants in Asia, McKinsey's office in India is growing faster than any others, and Boston Consulting Group earned $420 million of its $600 million revenues overseas.[25] Establishing such footholds gives these consultancies global presence, and the ability to react to client requirements no matter where they are in the world. It also recognizes that it is better to have locals developing and maintaining relationships with clients, than foreign nationals who typically have less understanding of the cultural environment in which they find themselves working.

The underlying attributes of national cultures are not generally accessible to the outsider. However, for those organizations that send their staff overseas for long-term assignments and secondments, there is usually some kind of cultural preparation. This normally excludes consultancies that seem to depend on the flexibility of their consultants to cope with the cultural variations; few provide any form of cultural training that sensitizes their staff to the differences between their own culture and those of the countries in which they are expected to work.

Fortunately, the work of Geert Hofstede[26] has shed some light on such variations, and when used with care can provide a degree of sensitivity that would otherwise be missing. Without going into immense detail, it is worth summarizing the key elements of Hofstede's work on national culture.

Hofstede surveyed the opinions, attitudes and beliefs of IBM employees across 50 countries. The 116,000 people surveyed occupied similar management positions within IBM, and were the same in every aspect bar nationality. This allowed the variations associated with nationality to be drawn out more starkly. The survey, which was based upon earlier research and hypotheses, established four areas of differentiation:

- Power distance: Hofstede defined this as the extent to which the less powerful members of institutions and organizations within a country expect and accept that power is distributed unequally.[27] In practice this means the degree to which subordinates are willing to question their superiors and resist decisions. Such resistance is more prevalent in Western societies and less common in the Far East. Where the acceptance of inequality is greatest, paternalistic and autocratic management styles tend to dominate (as in Japan), whilst the opposite is true in those countries where inequality is less acceptable. Here, management tends to be more consultative. This is typical of the Low Countries.
- Individualism–collectivism: this refers to the extent to which people within a society are expected to fend for themselves and their immediate families. The more one is expected to fend for oneself, the more individualistic the society. The opposite of this is collectivism, where, from birth, people are integrated into strong, cohesive groups which tend to be maintained throughout life.[28] As is to be expected, in those societies that are more collective, decision making tends to be group-based, and as a consequence often slower (for example, the Nordic countries) than in those countries that are more individualistic (for example, the United States and the United Kingdom). This has implications for the formation of relationships between individuals, because it is this that creates the basis of trust. Because collective societies tend to be dominated by the family unit, those outside are automatically mistrusted until such time as they can earn the trust of the family. This explains why in some places, such as China and southern Italy, there are very few large organizations. The majority tend to be family owned. The same is true for North African countries. The opposite is normally true in individualistic societies where people are more willing to trust those they come into contact with. Consultants must bear in mind these variations when considering their relationship management activities with their clients (see Chapter 8 for more detail).
- Masculinity–femininity: in those societies that can be considered masculine, emphasis tends to be placed on achievement, ambition and success (for example, the United States), whilst in those countries that are more feminine, the emphasis is on quality of work and caring for others (for example, Finland, The Netherlands and Sweden). As expected, in those countries that are more masculine, working hours tend to be longer. Americans are working longer and harder – 25 million people now work more than 49 hours a week, with a large number working a lot more; 11 million spend 60 hours or more at work.[29] The same is true for the United Kingdom, which has the longest working hours in Europe; 91 per cent of British managers now work more than their contracted hours.[30] In the more feminine cultures, work is a means to an end, not the end itself.
- Uncertainty avoidance: this refers to the extent to which members of a culture feel threatened by uncertain or unknown circumstances.[31] In those countries where uncertainty

avoidance is high, people attempt to reduce it through structure, process and familiarity, so that events are clearly interpretable. This is true of Germany, Switzerland and France. In addition, where uncertainty avoidance is high, people are less likely to question superiors and tend to avoid situations that involve conflict. I have seen this first-hand whilst working on an international assignment. At a meeting that involved Swiss, American, United Kingdom and New Zealand nationals, it was the Swiss manager that could not cope with conflict and actually froze during one particularly heated debate. Only through someone else's intervention could the meeting regain some semblance of direction and control. In those countries that have a weak uncertainty avoidance, there tends to be less concern or need for strict rules: people are generally more self-governing, conflict is seen as non-threatening and an important part of the workplace, and individuals are generally more flexible. This is typical of the United States, the United Kingdom and Australia.

Hofstede complemented his work with tables showing the scores for each of the four dimensions. This can be a useful ready-reckoner for those working within or leading multinational teams. The key thing about the scores is that they should not be treated as absolute. Instead, it is the relative difference between the scores of two nationalities that is important. In the context of multinational teams, such differences can have major impacts on the success of the assignment.

The work of Mark Williams can also aid the consultant when working overseas and in multicultural teams.[32] He identified ten lenses of culture which affect the way people perceive others from different nationalities. The lenses can help the consultant understand the way they see differences in such things as race, culture and ethnicity, and can be used to generate an additional level of sensitivity beyond that established by Hofstede. Assessing where you stand against each of these lenses allows some of the pitfalls associated with cross-border working to be minimized. The ten lenses are:

1. assimilationist: those who want people to submerge their individual and cultural identities in favour of nationalistic and patriotic ideals
2. colourblind: those who see people as individuals and ignore race, colour, ethnicity and other external cultural factors
3. culturalcentrist: those who seek to improve the welfare of their cultural group by accentuating their history and identity
4. elitist: those who believe in the superiority of the upper class and embrace the importance of family roots, wealth and social status
5. integrationist: those who support the breaking down of all barriers between racial groups by merging people of different cultures together in communities and in the workplace
6. meritocratist: those who believe in the individualist credo of a country; if you have the abilities and work hard enough, you can compete with anyone to make your dreams come true
7. multiculturalist: those who celebrate the diversity of cultures and the contributions they make to national culture and history
8. seclusionist: those who feel strongly that they should protect themselves from racial, cultural and/or ethnic groups that diminish the character and quality of their group's experiences within the society
9. transcendent: those who focus on the human spirit, people's universal connection and shared humanity

10. victim/caretaker: those who feel that they are still suffering from the generational impact of previous oppression, and therefore deserve compensation from society and the dominant culture.

There are, of course plenty of books that discuss how to conduct business in virtually every nation on earth, and these often boil down to a list of dos and don'ts. Such books can be useful because they provide a basic understanding of the national culture they are about to encounter. Ultimately, however, there is no substitute for ensuring consultants are suitably prepared for their international assignments; consultancies should not rely on their employees' intellectual skills alone. Furthermore, NLP and emotional intelligence will not substitute for cultural intelligence at any level, and certainly not national. Thus, Hofstede's and Williams's work provides an ideal starting point for managing multicultural engagements.

A recent article in the *Financial Times* highlighted the importance of national cultures to the success of organizations.[33] The article concerned the fortunes of the German software company Brokat, whose attempts to become more like an American software company ended in disaster, with it filing for insolvency. It seems that its desire to distance itself from its cultural roots failed. Conversely, those that are true to their cultural roots seem to be more successful. For example, the three most successful software companies in Europe – Germany's SAP, France's Dassault and the United Kingdom's Sage – all conform to their national stereotypes. SAP's software is solidly engineered and allows companies to generate efficiencies by tying together back-office processes, Dassault allows its customers to make big cultural statements through its 3D design software and Sage provides accounting software for a nation of shopkeepers. Whilst such cultural consistency underwrites their success, none have rivalled the size or reach of the United States software corporations. Culture may well have a hand in this too, as the United States, unlike Europe has a homogeneous culture.

FUNCTIONAL CULTURES

Whilst it is often convenient to refer to the organization as if it has a single homogeneous culture, this is rarely the case, because this single culture will encapsulate a number of subcultures. Such heterogeneity results from the differentiation that exists within organizations as they establish different functions to perform specific work activity. It should be clear that cultural variations exist between finance, marketing, information technology and other organizational divisions. Such differences exist because of the physical separation of the functions, the training that employees receive, the types of work they perform and the conditions they work under.[34] For example, the finance department has a fundamentally different culture to the marketing department because it focuses on the financial health of the organization, whilst marketing focuses on the development and marketing of the organization's products, as well as establishing and promoting its brand. The skills, practices and policies valued in one area will not necessarily be valued in another. The challenge for most organizations is therefore to ensure that their organizational culture is strong enough to allow functions to co-operate over corporate issues.

Culture clashes

Because culture is complex and the behaviour of individuals within an organization is influenced by the nation in which they live, the organization that employs them and the function in which they work, clashes of culture should be anticipated by the consultant. Ultimately, of course, such clashes have a lot to do with the creation and exercising of power. And power is about inequalities, ownership of resources in its various forms, and control. It reflects the ability of individuals to exploit the inequalities that exist within organizations to gain advantage, and hence power over their rivals. This perspective reflects that put forward by Machiavelli in his book *The prince*:[35] in writing about sixteenth-century court life, he observed the locus of power at any one time reflected the contingent nature of the situation, the people and their interaction. Power was continuously produced and reproduced, and the retention of power, once gained, required immense effort and constant vigilance. Maintaining power within the modern corporation is not as violent as it was back then, but it certainly requires some of the subtleties described by Machiavelli. For example, whilst people may compete for position and power within a single department, as members of the same department they are also involved within a wider power game with other departments. Resource scarcities and turbulent business environments create the same shift of power described by Machiavelli, in which organizational functions jockey for dominance by aligning themselves to the key issues facing the board of directors. Thus, over time, the relative power of functions will ebb and flow as the key issues facing the board change. The implications of this for the consultant's work should not be underestimated, as it will give rise to politics and power plays during the engagement. I will discuss power and politics in more detail in Chapters 7 and 8.

Given that projects and programmes exacerbate inter-functional and cultural rivalries and that consultants are typically involved with cross-functional change, a rough ride should usually be expected – at least in the short term. This is principally because incremental change associated with ongoing process improvements is insufficient to maintain business viability. Organizations have realized that projects are the most effective means of introducing radical and rapid change. But there is a price – civil war. Projects and programmes of change will bring out the worst in inter-functional (and hence cultural) conflict. And that is one reason why consultants are brought in – they will drive home the change in an objective and corporate way without getting too embroiled in the politics and power plays. Naturally, politics and power should not be ignored, as they still have to be managed. But the key thing is that the consultants are working on behalf of the entire organization, not one of the embattled functions.

Unless working across international boundaries, cultural problems typically occur at functional level, and include:

- The differences in functional language. This can be a perfect way to confuse the consultant and ensure that they don't fully understand the functional issues.
- The use of information as a source of power. The ability to control information that is important to the organization has become an important form of power. This has been reinforced by the bloodletting resulting from the business–process re-engineering projects of the early to mid-1990s, and the phenomenal growth in information. For example, in 1990 the typical Fortune 500 company stored 33 billion characters of electronic data, and in 2010 this is expected to be 400 trillion.[36] Thus incorrect, out of date or deliberately distorted information may be passed to the engagement team, leading to wrong conclusions and recommendations. This behaviour can be driven out of resistance to change, as much as the function seeking dominance within the organization.
- The hijacking of projects and programmes by powerful functions. If the consultant is not

careful to manage the politics surrounding the engagement, or begins to lose their objectivity, there is a real danger of being overly influenced by one function or another.

The two specific types of cultural issues faced during international engagements include:

- Intercultural problems between different nationalities. These problems can be a major issue for engagements, because of the differences in decision making, attitudes to work, timekeeping, relationships with superiors and so on. This can happen when working in mixed nationality teams and for overseas clients. It is generally easier to adjust to a client than a mixed team, especially if large. For example, when working with a Sudanese client, I found their approach to communication and timekeeping was very different to my own. But, instead of trying to impose additional discipline, I accepted that time was less pressing than in the United Kingdom. This proved to be the best strategy, and ensured the assignment was a success. Sensitizing the consultant to the likely issues is essential and can be achieved through training professional staff in the issues associated with intercultural management and co-operation.
- Power plays between regions. This can occur in any global organization, and can be considered to be a higher-order form of functional warfare. The main issue here is that the intercultural aspects come into play as well. I have experienced this first-hand when running a global programme for an investment bank. Managing the United States region was fine as long as I specified my requirements precisely. When these were vague, they would pursue their own agenda. The Swiss region needed a lot of hand-holding and required strong leadership to ensure they completed the programme of work. The British were probably the worst to manage as the majority of those involved were unconcerned with what had to be achieved – they were more interested in their own agendas.

Summary

In this chapter we have briefly covered the foundation to cultural intelligence: culture. There is little doubt that culture is an important and essential component of any organization. As well as being a critical element to success, culture can present major obstacles to organizations when they are changing, particularly during mergers and acquisitions. It should be clear that being attuned to the national, organizational and functional variations in culture is a vital skill for the consultant. And the key to making the consultant culturally intelligent lies in providing them with a model of culture that they can readily understand and apply. This model is the focus of the final chapter of Part I.

3 Introducing the cultural intelligence model

The burden, however, is still on the advisor to quickly understand each individual client's preferred style of interaction, and to be sufficiently flexible to deal with him or her in a manner that the client finds most comfortable and effective. The one thing that the advisor must not do is to commit to a single consultative style and say 'Well, that's my style. The clients can take it or leave it'. That really would be pompous, patronizing, and arrogant.[1]

This quote from *The trusted advisor* sums up the philosophy behind cultural intelligence: there is no one best way of delivering the consultancy proposition, and it is absolutely essential to take into account the client's style (culture) when deciding on how the assignment is to be sold, executed and managed. All too often consultancies subscribe to the methodological approach to delivery, which for many clients is destined for disaster irrespective of the success of the engagement. This not only applies to the execution of an engagement, but also to how the sale is executed and the relationship between consultant and client is developed.

The impact of poor cultural intelligence – Westpac's CS90[2]

When the Australian banking system was deregulated in 1984, the existing banks were forced to take a hard look at the way they did business because deregulation meant the invasion of foreign banks. It also meant increased opportunities to compete locally and globally. Westpac saw information technology, and lots of it, as the weapon that would allow them to do so. Its high-profile entry into the electronic financial services sector was called Core Systems 90 (CS90), and when it was publicly launched in August 1987 expectations were high. CS90 had an initial cost of around A$100 million and a completion date in the late 1980s, but in 1992, still two years from completion and A$50 million over budget, the project was terminated and 500 employees sacked.

CS90 was always a very ambitious project which at its core was a suite of five applications and a set of development tools. The idea was that the applications and the development tools would be proved in-house and then sold worldwide. From a technical perspective, CS90 was always feasible. Westpac had problems, however, in adapting its corporate culture to the demands of CS90, and although the initial marketing of CS90 to staff went well, it was not sustained. At first staff were enthusiastic about the potential benefits, but once the development staff started to delve into the costs of individual bank products the relationship broke down because of politics and the feeding of incorrect data to the development staff by the user communities. The IT staff also had major problems in trying to simultaneously create an in-house system as well as a commercially viable product for which there was an obvious global market.

Westpac went into partnership with IBM, which supplied the hardware and design expertise for the project. Problems immediately arose because of the major differences in culture between the two organizations. Much of the difficulty stemmed from IBM's use of staff who were more familiar with defence projects and in dealing with United States government departments. And, despite providing Westpac staff with two-day training courses geared to understanding the language and approaches used by IBM consultants, problems between the two cultures proved intractable. An additional problem occurred when IBM attempted to graft extremely rigid and complex system development requirements and processes to the CS90 project. Although such discipline was necessary for the defence industry, it was much too detailed and restrictive for the bank. In particular, the methods proved incapable of dealing with the fast and furious nature of banking. The Westpac corporate environment was also intolerant of mistakes, so when the project went late and over budget, CS90 management were forced to hype the project's benefits to keep funds flowing until its eventual failure in 1992.

WHAT WENT WRONG

The failure of CS90 was the result of many factors, not least those linked to the way in which the project was executed, and the way the bank conducted its day-to-day business. However, there were significant factors associated with the client–consultant relationship with IBM, including:

- failure to prepare before the engagement, especially in relation to:
  - not taking the time to understand the nature of investment and retail banks in their widest sense
  - failing to consider the adjustments in style necessary to adapt to the mercenary culture of Westpac; IBM staff were more used to the fragmented culture of government organizations
  - failing to review their development methods and approaches which were geared toward meeting stringent Department of Defense quality standards rather than the generally process-free needs of the bank
  - failing to integrate into the wider project team. Instead they managed to isolate themselves and the project team from the rest of the bank. Again, this may have been acceptable within defence projects, but was totally unsuitable for Westpac where accountability and visibility were essential. In particular, IBM forced the client to adjust, rather than the other way around, which displayed an appalling level of arrogance
- failing to apply basic client-facing skills when the project started to falter.

Westpac illustrates just how wrong an engagement can go when the consultancy fails to consider the cultural dimension to its work. But in less extreme cases, such cultural errors can result in client dissatisfaction, consultants' being asked to leave the assignment, inappropriate solutions, extra work for the engagement manager, unnecessary turbulence and the loss of future work.

The benefits of cultural intelligence

In order to illustrate the benefits of cultural intelligence, consider the following vignette which describes the experience of a Japanese company that was bidding against

American, British and German consortiums for the design and build of a chemical plant in Germany.[3]

Although the Japanese bid was not the cheapest, or the most technically superior, it won the contract to the surprise of the remaining bidders, who at this time were the Americans and the British; the Germans had failed at the first hurdle. Both the Americans and the British appealed against the decision, and, unusually, the client invited them to discuss why they had lost the bid. Although both bids were of the highest quality, considered technically superior, and presented extremely professionally, they failed for one reason, and one reason only – client focus. The Japanese had taken the trouble to conduct all their dealings with the client in German, including the final presentation. This meant that, as well as producing the bid, members of the Japanese consortium had taken the trouble to learn German and ensure they fully understood the cultural aspects of their client. As a result they were able to satisfy the technical aspects of the bid, but more importantly were able to demonstrate empathy and understanding of the client, their business issues and culture – a winning combination. Although it is not always necessary to conduct business in the client's mother tongue, it is important to understand their culture.

I believe the benefits of cultural intelligence to the consulting community and their clients to be significant. If applied across the complete consulting life cycle it allows:

- the account team to devise a suitable strategy to open and farm the account
- the sales pitch to be tailored according to the client's prevailing culture – therefore, as well as bringing all the technical understanding associated with the client's market and the solution being proposed, the consultants would be able to position the presentation according to the specifics of the culture
- the engagement team to be fully prepared before setting foot on the client site: the team would have a basic understanding of the client's culture and what it meant for how the engagement would operate
- those responsible for relationship management to develop a suitable strategy that concentrates on the way relationships work within the client.

Cultural intelligence reduces the levels of stress experienced by the consultants and client. Stress is at its most extreme at the start of an engagement when consultants are trying to deliver something of immediate value, are adjusting to the client's culture and are attempting to cope with the high levels of definitional uncertainty. Stress levels usually increase sharply until the team has settled in with the client and the outcomes of the engagement finally become clear. At this stage stress levels remain fairly constant apart from variations caused by crises and problems that will arise from time to time. Then, assuming the engagement comes to a successful end the levels of stress will reduce sharply, until the consultants move to their next engagement, when the whole process starts again.

The cultural intelligence tools

In order to avoid the types of problems faced at the Westpac engagement and to realize the benefits of cultural intelligence highlighted above, it is necessary to provide the consultant with a basic set of tools with which to develop the required sensitivities. The remainder of this chapter describes two tools that can be used by the consultant to assess a client's organizational culture and their dominant behaviours. Together these provide a guide for adapting sales, engagements and relationships to the target client's culture. Part II will focus on the impact this model has on the major consulting process.

The culture assessment tool

The model of organizational culture introduced in this section was originally developed by Rob Goffee and Gareth Jones and described in their book *The character of a corporation* (1998). The model and associated culture questionnaire and scoring mechanism have been reproduced with permission from HarperCollins.

The Goffee and Jones model was chosen because of its simplicity and accessibility. When we consider that there are literally hundreds of definitions of culture with many alternative models, anyone interested in applying culture to a practical situation would be hard pushed to settle on one that was widely applicable. Moreover, with the consultancy profession relying on straightforward tools and frameworks, firms and consultants alike would reject anything that was overly complex. Therefore choosing a model of culture that could be readily understood (through the use of suitable metaphors) was essential if it was to be accepted by consultancies. The Goffee and Jones model is one of the few I have come across that falls into this category. It is based upon two underlying dimensions: sociability and solidarity.

SOCIABILITY

Sociability is a measure of friendliness among members of a community, whether inside or outside work. In both forms, sociability shows that people within a community care for others. Thus, just as families and friends exchange cards and socialize, so do work colleagues. There are many advantages to high levels of sociability: it makes the working environment a pleasure for the employees; it promotes high morale and a strong *esprit de corps*; it fosters teamwork and creativity; and it creates an environment in which individuals are willing to go the extra mile for their colleagues and ultimately their firm – they usually work until the job is done rather than following a strict nine-to-five work pattern. However, just as there is a light side to high levels of sociability, there is a dark side which can have major drawbacks for the firm, including: allowing poor performance to be hidden from view when colleagues make up for the deficiencies in others, exaggerating concern for consensus when making decisions, and allowing cliques and informal networks to form that can be used to circumvent and undermine due process.

SOLIDARITY

Solidarity is based upon the achievement of tasks which involve people who share common interests. To ensure success, these tasks must have clearly articulated goals and targets associated with them, and must provide direct links to personal benefits (such as bonuses, pay rises and career progression). The key difference between solidarity and sociability is that these tasks can be achieved without people liking each other. High solidarity organizations often have a ruthless and disciplined focus on their objectives, something that staff, shareholders and customers like. In such organizations sociability often comes a poor second to getting the job done. Although this may not be a bad thing, one of the biggest problems with high solidarity organizations is that the singular focus on goals can be at the expense of those who get in the way; it's do or die, and dog eat dog. Such an environment can be very hard to accept for those who prefer more social working conditions.

The culture of the organization is thus defined by the combination of these two dimensions and leads to the four generic cultures described below and illustrated in Figure 3.1.

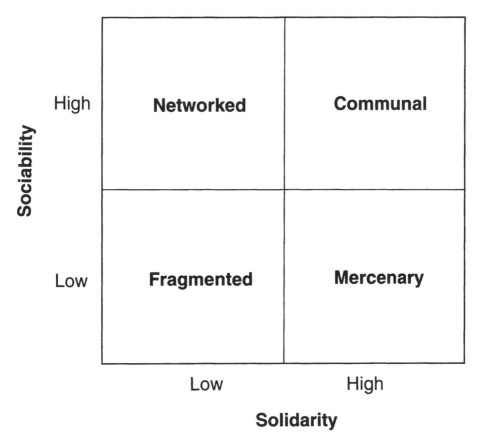

Figure 3.1   The four cultures

THE NETWORKED CULTURE

The networked culture is typically one that exudes friendship and kindness. People genuinely like each other, and display high levels of empathy. There also tends to be a high degree of trust between them. The networked organization is typically conversational, with people entering into discussions that cover all topics, from work to what they did over the weekend. This emphasis on friendship displays itself in the value placed on patience and tolerance as people are able to have their say without getting talked down. The office space tends to be personalized and an open-door policy predominates. Time is taken to socialize both within work and outside it. The communication process tends to be both formalized, through face-to-face discussions and in meetings, and informal, as part of the general socializing outside the workplace. Examples of organizations with networked cultures include Unilever, Heineken and Philips.[4]

THE MERCENARY CULTURE

The mercenary culture is restless and ruthless, with a powerful drive to get things done. Goals tend to be at the forefront in people's minds, as they strive to make things happen. Time between coming up with an idea and executing it is short; time is everything, as is action. Winning is very important to the mercenary organization, and those within it. Mercenary organizations achieve their external goals by setting very high internal ones, using goals, targets and objectives to get there. Communication is swift and to the point. Getting the job done may entail long hours, as leaving before the job is finished is usually frowned upon. Value is placed on reacting quickly and not overdoing the thinking time. Examples include Citicorp, PepsiCo and Mars.[5] The following two extracts from David Cohen's book *Fear, greed and panic* illustrate the nature of the mercenary culture very well:[6]

> Simon thinks he was not such a good trader. You need to be totally assertive and instantly assertive – and he thinks he just wasn't assertive enough. It's instant assertiveness that's wanted. It's also important not to brood.

> 'It takes a lot of physical stamina, of waiting just standing around for something to happen.' Nigel Glen added he knew of one trader who was 27 who had had three heart attacks. 'I think that says stress,' he added. Simon pointed out Liffe is brutal. Other dealers soon know if you are doing well or badly. Failure is very public – and failure means you've failed to understand the market at that moment.

THE COMMUNAL CULTURE

The communal culture is one that combines the friendship associated with the networked culture and the drive and ambition of the mercenary culture. Passion for the company and its products go hand in hand with a strong sense of community and shared responsibility. Organizations that fall into the communal culture tend to have a work hard, play hard ethos about them that is highly infectious. Office space tends to be shared, and there are few barriers between functions. Communication is everywhere, with every channel being used (meetings, face-to-face, corridors and so on). Work and non-work life meld into one, with work becoming a way of life. More importantly, people live and breathe the organization and its mission; they are almost evangelical about it. Examples include Hewlett-Packard and Johnson & Johnson.[7] Another includes Oakley, the company that sells branded sunglasses:

> Oakley is a model of self-belief. Not only does the company sell a brand of idiosyncratic self-confidence in the form of distinctive bow-shaped sunglasses, but its entire working culture reflects that same pride. It was set up back in 1975 with a determination to be youth-driven and original and has maintained that emphasis despite growing rapidly ever since. They work the way their customers live.[8]

Some recent research by McKinsey as part of its investigations into the war for talent shed some light on the type of culture that most people would like to work within. Although it found that people preferred different types of corporate cultures, two dimensions stood out very strongly, a strong performance orientation and an open and trusting environment. In fact 94 per cent of the managers surveyed wanted this combination. This places the communal culture at the heart of most people's cultural aspirations. The reality is that there are comparatively few communal organizations around, as all too often market focus and mistrust tend to creep in and distort the culture. What people want and what they have to deal with are clearly two different things,[9] which may help to explain why so many people would like to change jobs. A recent survey by the career consultancy Penna, Sanders & Sidney found that two-thirds of employees would change jobs tomorrow if they could.[10]

THE FRAGMENTED CULTURE

Within the fragmented culture people are not particularly friendly toward each other, and they do not support the organization or its goals; they work at an organization, but primarily for themselves. People tend to favour working in isolation and uninterruptedly. As a result, doors tend to be closed, and offices well equipped for self-contained work. Work is often conducted at home or on the road, rather than in the office; being away from the office is usually a sign that the employee is busy (for example, with clients). People tend to associate more with their profession than the organization. Communication is usually work related, and brief. And, because people are often absent, few meetings take place. A good example of the fragmented culture is Chrysler, which in the late 1970s exhibited many of the dysfunctional qualities of the fragmented culture:

> Chrysler didn't really function like a company at all. Chrysler in 1978 was like Italy in the 1860s – the company consisted of a cluster of little duchies, each run by a prima donna. It was a bunch of mini-empires with nobody giving a damn about what anyone else was doing.[11]

The real power of the Goffee and Jones model lies in its ability to describe four basic organizational cultures without needing to go into esoteric descriptions. Moreover, because it describes the cultures so well, it is easy to pin individual observations against it. This is very useful to the consultant who has to assimilate vast amounts of information about the engagement and the client in a short space of time. Therefore having a framework that allows an understanding of the basic client culture ensures that the consultant hits the ground running, at least from the perspective of how to behave once on site. Chapter 6 will address this in detail.

ASSESSING CLIENT CULTURE

Assessing a client culture in its basic form is achieved using a three-step process:

- step 1: complete the questionnaire (Table 3.1)
- step 2: total up the scores (Figure 3.2)
- step 3: plot the results (Figure 3.3).

Step 1 – complete the questionnaire

The questionnaire is designed to be completed by those who have knowledge of the organization under assessment. For consultants attempting to develop a relationship with a client for the first time, this can be a problem. However, it is normal for the account team to establish relationships with the client some time before a sale is made. Therefore, the questionnaire can be used as part of the relationship management process to gain a better

Table 3.1   Assessing an organization's culture

Questions	Strongly disagree	Disagree	Neither agree nor disagree	Agree	Strongly agree
1. The group I am assessing (organization, division, unit, or team) knows its business objectives clearly.	1	2	3	4	5
2. People genuinely like one another.	1	2	3	4	5
3. People follow clear guidelines and instructions about work.	1	2	3	4	5
4. People get along very well and disputes are rare.	1	2	3	4	5
5. Poor performance is dealt with quickly and firmly.	1	2	3	4	5
6. People often socialize outside of work.	1	2	3	4	5
7. The group really wants to win.	1	2	3	4	5
8. People do favours for each other because they like one another.	1	2	3	4	5
9. When opportunities for competitive advantage arise people move decisively to capitalize on them.	1	2	3	4	5
10. People make friends for the sake of friendship – there is no other agenda.	1	2	3	4	5
11. Strategic goals are shared.	1	2	3	4	5
12. People often confide in one another about personal matters.	1	2	3	4	5
13. People build close long-term relationships – someday they might be of benefit.	1	2	3	4	5
14. Reward and punishment are clear.	1	2	3	4	5
15. People know a lot about each other's families.	1	2	3	4	5
16. The group is determined to beat clearly defined enemies.	1	2	3	4	5
17. People are always encouraged to work things out flexibly – as they go along.	1	2	3	4	5
18. Hitting targets is the single most important thing.	1	2	3	4	5
19. To get something done you can work around the system.	1	2	3	4	5
20. Projects that are started are complete.	1	2	3	4	5
21. When people leave, co-workers stay in contact to see how they are doing.	1	2	3	4	5
22. It is clear where one person's job ends and another person's begins.	1	2	3	4	5
23. People protect each other.	1	2	3	4	5

understanding of the client. This is something the client will appreciate because the consultants are taking a genuine interest in their organization. More detail of how this is done will be provided in Chapters 5 and 8. In those instances where consultants are already on site the process is generally easier, as relationships already exist.

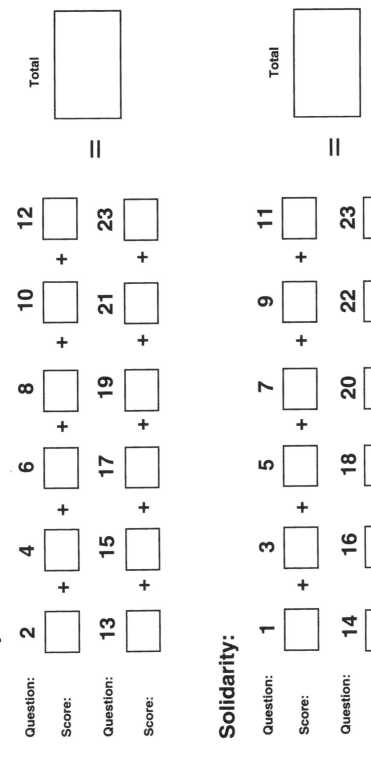

Figure 3.2 Scoring the results

47

When completing the questionnaire it is important to bear in mind three things. First, you need to ensure that you are clear on the organizational level you are assessing, as the results are likely to vary. For example, the corporate culture may be different from the functional cultures. Second, the results should be viewed as a guide rather than an absolute. Once on site, observation will allow the results to be confirmed or adjusted where required. The purpose of the questionnaire is to begin to develop a sensitivity to client culture, not to define it precisely. Third, it is best to have the questionnaire completed by enough people to provide confidence in the results. In general, five should yield a sufficiently accurate indication of the culture. When answering the questionnaire indicate how strongly you agree or disagree with the 23 statements by ringing the number (1 to 5) that corresponds to your answer.

Step 2 – total up the scores

Having completed the questionnaire, the next step is to assess the level of sociability and solidarity by adding up the scores from the questions as shown in Figure 3.2. The numbers above the boxes correspond to the questions in Table 3.1. Therefore, if the answer to question 2 is 5, write 5 in the box with the number 2 above it.

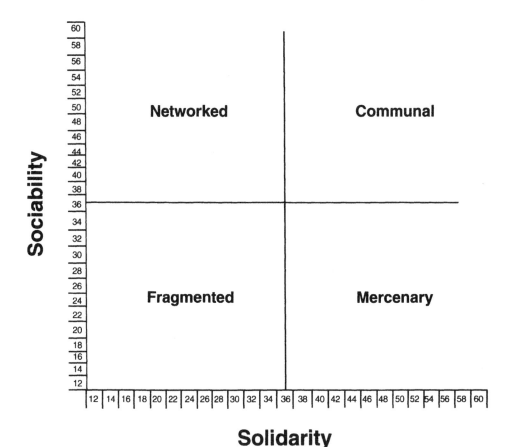

Figure 3.3 Which client culture?

Step 3 – plot the results

The final step is to plot the results on the matrix (Figure 3.3) which will indicate the dominant culture for the organization or function under assessment.

INTERPRETING THE RESULTS

Depending on the coverage of the assessment, the results will either fall within a single quadrant or across more than one. In the former, this suggests that the organization or function under assessment has a strong and dominant culture. In this instance, the description of the culture introduced earlier can be used to formulate the consultancy response and for preparing the consultancy team prior to walking on site. In the latter, it may reflect a more heterogeneous culture and one where the organization's functional cultures vary considerably. In this case, the response from the consultancy will have to be more complex. It may also reflect a cross-functional view and as a result it might be necessary to seek further clarification by having other clients/consultants complete the questionnaire. More detail on how to apply the results of the questionnaire will be given in Part II.

Of course, it is possible to make generalizations about the types of organizations that fall within each of the four cultures as well as those that fall into specific market sectors (Figure 3.4). This is possible because the nature of the operating environments and the primary market forces that affect the organization help to determine and reinforce an organization's culture. It would follow therefore that those organizations that operate within harsh market conditions are more likely to be mercenary. This would include investment banks, which must be capable of fast and decisive action in order to react to changes in the financial markets and manufacturers, which in turn have to react quickly to changes in economic conditions, as well as demanding clients and the implications of low margins. For those organizations that are new, such as the dotcoms, they are likely to be communal – small enough to have a real sense of community, and passionate enough about their new business to put the hours in to make it successful. Some organizations manage to retain their communal culture as they grow. For example, Gore Associates, a privately held, multimillion-dollar high tech firm based in Newark, Delaware, is a well-established company that behaves like a small entrepreneurial start-up. Gore has managed to create a small company ethos so infectious and sticky that it has survived its growth into a billion-dollar company with thousands of employees.[12] The higher-order professional organizations that attract those who pride themselves on personal knowledge and client relationships tend to be fragmented. In particular, academic, legal and sales organizations fall into this category. And although silo mentality rules, it does not necessarily affect the success of the organization as a whole. Mainstream organizations, such as those that operate in stable and well-established markets, tend to be networked. This is typical of the retail banking community and insurance organizations. Although such organizations are still subject to shock events – such as regulatory intervention (as with utilities), mergers, acquisitions and hostile take-overs (as within retail banking and insurance) – they are very resilient.

UNDERSTANDING BOUNDARY CONDITIONS

Like any generalizations, there will always be exceptions. For example, whereas most investment banks can be considered mercenary, the online investor Schwab is far more networked than most of its competitors. Equally, there are pockets of government that can be consid-

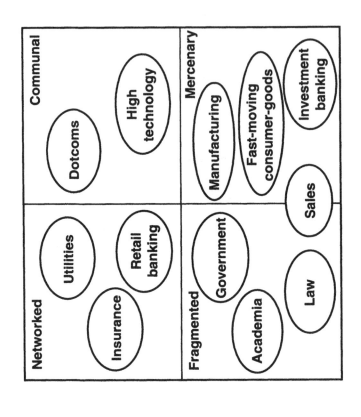

Networked	Communal
Established firms operating within stable markets	New and innovative firms
Fragmented	**Mercenary**
High-end professional services and pure sales organizations	Fast-moving and/or low-margin companies

Figure 3.4 Cultural generalizations

ered to be more mercenary than the norm. For example, the appointment of a chief executive with investment banking experience at the UK's Customs & Excise is likely to alter the underlying culture to one that is more outcome-focused and mercenary. Another example is Tesco, the UK supermarket retailer, which according to the generalized view of culture should be mercenary (because it is a fast-moving consumer-goods organization). However, because of its history, and the way in which it dislodged Sainsbury, its arch-rival, from the number one slot, it sits along the boundary of the communal and mercenary cultures. Tesco has an unusual self-belief in its capabilities, whilst still retaining the mercenary edge to its activities. These examples suggest that there are boundary conditions where the rule of thumb breaks down and the organization will display elements of more than one culture. This suggests that, although generalizations are possible, it is always advisable to test any assumptions by using the questionnaire and checking personal observations against the descriptions of the cultures. Using the descriptions of the culture will also help the consultant make an assessment as to the likelihood of clients' falling within the boundary of two cultures.

WHERE CONSULTANCIES FIT IN

Consultancies occupy a unique position in the model, as most tend to sit in more than one of the four cultures. From the firm's perspective, two cultures dominate: networked and fragmented. This is particularly true of large partnerships. The partners are typically fragmented and the professional staff networked because they have to work well together to get the job done. This has implications for the way consultants relate to the senior executives in their firm. It is important to work with each partner as an individual, rather like working with a fragmented client. However, such cultural variations do not stop there, as firms will also tend to fall into one of two camps – those that fall within a single culture, and those that usually cover all four. The former tend to be specialist consultancies focusing on a specific sector, such as government, finance or manufacturing, whilst the latter can either be a boutique consultancy, such as a strategy house, providing a service across all industry sectors or a combination of service and industry specialisms, such as the Big Four. Despite the differences in focus, the majority of consultancies tend to have an underlying networked culture, as progress to the senior levels not only depends on the ability to deliver high-value assignments, but also to be well known around the firm. Within the larger consultancies that have a mix of industry specialists and services, there also tends to be significant variations in local culture. For the consultants that specialize within one sector, say corporate finance, the practice in which they work normally mirrors the culture of their clients. This is not surprising given that such consultants would have been recruited from the industry sector in the first place. Because these specialists normally work exclusively within one sector, they are rarely exposed to other client cultures. When they are, however, there can be issues for both the consultancy and the client, as we saw in the case of Westpac. The service specialists can be considered to be more generalist because they move from organization to organization, sector to sector, as they deliver their assignments. Consultants that fall into this category include those with specific technical skills, such as a knowledge of enterprise resource planning systems, project management, strategy, programme management and so on. And, because the service specialists move from culture to culture, it follows that they should be more culturally intelligent than their specialist industry colleagues.

REFINING CULTURAL UNDERSTANDING – COMMON BEHAVIOURS

As we have seen, each of the four cultures has its indicators. But in order to provide the consultant with some additional help, the basic model has been augmented with a behavioural questionnaire designed to assess five dominant behaviours within organizations: time, control, survival, risk and trust.

Time

The time dimension is all about how people and the organization perceive time, and how they behave based on this perception. In organizations that feel constrained by time, there is more focus on action than thinking, with people expected to deliver results as quickly as possible. Quality of results is often of secondary importance to fast delivery. People tend to be rushed and energetic, with decisions being made on the fly. In general, little time is spent planning prior to taking action. In organizations that can be considered to be time-rich, there is a greater emphasis on consensus building and careful planning. As a result, feedback tends to be slower and more considered, and progress on projects much slower. People are less rushed, and the quality of results is considered to be more important than the speed of delivery. Because people are not rushed, finishing work to prescribed deadlines is not considered important, and there are rarely sanctions for late delivery.

Control

Control is all about establishing and maintaining predictability within the working environment. In organizations that value tight control, there is an emphasis on process and procedures. These tend to be detailed, and it is expected that people will follow these to the letter. In these organizations, people tend to behave formally and there is little tolerance for mavericks. In organizations that have loose control, planning is not seen as a value-adding activity, and people are trusted to complete the work as they see fit. In loose control organizations, people behave informally with each other, and work tends to be far more unstructured and fluid. There is little process, and where there is, this is only used if it adds value to the task in hand. There also tends to be a greater tolerance toward different working styles and behaviours; mavericks are acceptable, so long as they deliver.

Survival

Survival is all about how people get on within the organization, and how they should behave in order to move up the hierarchy. It is also about how the organization as a whole survives in the wider market place. In the results-focused organization, survival is about achievement, and the recognition of getting the job done. People will tend to seek out demanding projects in which they can display their value as a means of progression. Conversely, in those organizations where survival is all about sponsorship, a person's ability to get on depends on how well they are networked into the organization and how they are perceived by the wider peer group and senior management communities, especially by those who have power and influence. Without sponsorship, people will not progress. At the organizational level, organizations that continuously reinvent themselves perceive innovation as the key way of surviving a turbulent environment. Such organizations will seek out value and ruthlessly exploit it. But because achievement is important, they will be willing to change with the market. They may even try to drive the market. In organizations which rely on tradition, innovation tends to be limited, as they tend to prefer stable, not turbulent, markets, and rely heavily on their reputation and brand.

Risk

Risk is all about considering the impacts of decisions and actions on the individual and organization. In risk-averse organizations, care is taken to consider all risks before acting, and as a result the decision-making process will be slow, as time will be taken to get as much information as possible about the subject before acting. Innovation tends to be limited, and people tend to follow prescribed ways of working. Following process is considered the best way of managing risk. Risk-averse organizations also tend to favour tight controls, as this ensures a consistent and hence less risky outcome. Within organizations that are risk-seeking, people do not fully consider risks before acting. In general the organization tends to be more willing to react to events, preferring to act and then consider the implications later. Being nimble is very important, so process tends to be light where it is used, and in many cases is absent all together. People are expected to take risks. The key point is understanding the difference between knowing and doing, and closing the gap as fast as possible. In the risk-averse organization there is an understanding that something should be done, but the risks prevent action from being taken. In the risk-seeking organization, the converse is true.

Trust

Trust is all about how people work together and how willing they are to share information. In high-trust organizations, people openly discuss issues and collaborate on projects. There is a general bias towards teamwork and working for the good of the organization. In the low-trust organization, people tend to work alone, protect their patch fiercely, and openly criticize their colleagues and management. People are generally concerned about getting stabbed in the back, and as a result they tend to be always looking for someone to blame. Politics tends to be rife in the low-trust organizations, but not always obvious to the casual observer. Ironically, many consultancies suffer from this type of problem, and this often prevents them from adding as much value as they could. In the end petty rivalries get in the way of client service.

The behaviour assessment tool

ASSESSING CLIENT BEHAVIOUR

Like culture, assessing client behaviour is achieved using a three-step process:

- step 1: complete the behaviour questionnaire (Table 3.2)
- step 2: total up the scores (Figure 3.5)
- step 3: plot the results (Figure 3.6).

Step 1 – complete the questionnaire

As with the previous questionnaire, it is best to complete this with either the help of the client or fellow consultants with knowledge and experience of the client being assessed. As before it is a good idea to have a minimum of five people complete it to get a general feel for the dominance of the five behaviours. When answering the questionnaire indicate how strongly you agree or disagree with the 30 statements by circling the number (1 to 5) that corresponds to the question.

Table 3.2 Assessing client behaviour

Questions	Strongly disagree	Disagree	Neither agree nor disagree	Agree	Strongly agree
1. People trust each other to get the job done.	1	2	3	4	5
2. Time is always seen as a constraint.	1	2	3	4	5
3. When things go wrong, people do not look for someone to blame.	1	2	3	4	5
4. People prefer to react to events.	1	2	3	4	5
5. Taking risks is valued.	1	2	3	4	5
6. People are empowered to take responsibility for their work.	1	2	3	4	5
7. Methods and processes are strictly followed.	1	2	3	4	5
8. People are concerned about their status.	1	2	3	4	5
9. People usually work in groups.	1	2	3	4	5
10. People will not speak out with management present.	1	2	3	4	5
11. The work environment is highly structured.	1	2	3	4	5
12. People rarely take time out from their work to talk.	1	2	3	4	5
13. Decisions are made quickly.	1	2	3	4	5
14. Control is centralized.	1	2	3	4	5
15. The organization reinvents itself.	1	2	3	4	5
16. Functions collaborate freely.	1	2	3	4	5
17. Process is used only where it adds value.	1	2	3	4	5
18. People behave formally.	1	2	3	4	5
19. The organization prefers short-term solutions.	1	2	3	4	5
20. Costs are tracked and controlled very carefully.	1	2	3	4	5
21. People are allowed to fail.	1	2	3	4	5
22. Tradition is important.	1	2	3	4	5
23. Time is rarely spent looking at what the competition is doing.	1	2	3	4	5
24. Predictability in outcomes is unimportant.	1	2	3	4	5
25. People feel fully briefed about what is happening in the organization.	1	2	3	4	5
26. People get on by who they know, not what they know.	1	2	3	4	5
27. The organization and the people within it are open to newcomers.	1	2	3	4	5
28. People are not concerned about the risks when taking action.	1	2	3	4	5
29. People are in a rush to get things done.	1	2	3	4	5
30. Risks are rarely identified before taking action.	1	2	3	4	5

Step 2 – total up the scores

Having completed the questionnaire, the next step is to assess how strong the five behaviours are by adding up the scores (Figure 3.5) from the questions set out in Table 3.2. Once again the number above the box corresponds to the question of Table 3.2, and the score for that question (1 to 5) should be written in the box below the question.

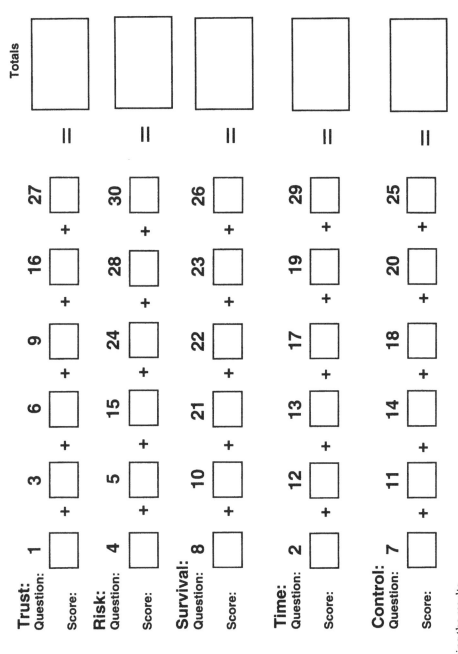

Trust:
Question: 1 + 3 + 6 + 9 + 16 + 27 = ☐

Score: ☐ + ☐ + ☐ + ☐ + ☐ + ☐

Risk:
Question: 4 + 5 + 15 + 24 + 28 + 30 = ☐

Score: ☐ + ☐ + ☐ + ☐ + ☐ + ☐

Survival:
Question: 8 + 10 + 21 + 22 + 23 + 26 = ☐

Score: ☐ + ☐ + ☐ + ☐ + ☐ + ☐

Time:
Question: 2 + 12 + 13 + 17 + 19 + 29 = ☐

Score: ☐ + ☐ + ☐ + ☐ + ☐ + ☐

Control:
Question: 7 + 11 + 14 + 18 + 20 + 25 = ☐

Score: ☐ + ☐ + ☐ + ☐ + ☐ + ☐

Totals

Figure 3.5 Scoring the results

55

Step 3 – plot the results

The final step is to plot the results on the model (Figure 3.6).

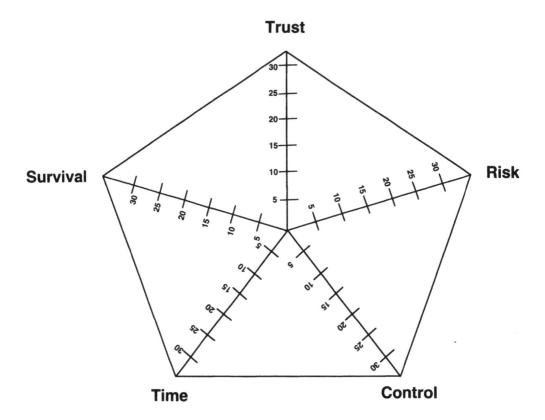

Figure 3.6   Which behaviours count?

INTERPRETING THE RESULTS

Table 3.3 describes the characteristics of the extremes of each of the five behaviours. Where the results fall in the middle of the two extremes, it is likely that the organization will display elements of both.

When considering the results of the questionnaire, it is also useful to place them in the context of the four cultures defined at the beginning of the chapter, as each of the five behaviours will vary according to the underlying organizational culture (Figure 3.7). Therefore, within mercenary cultures time will be at a premium, people will generally take risks, especially those whose bonuses depend on it, control is often tight to ensure things get done and survival is based on achieving objectives. Although there is an element of sponsorship in such organizations, progress (survival) is about getting the job done. The biggest issue within mercenary cultures is the general lack of trust. People are not generally trusted, which explains why the blame culture dominates. When things go wrong, someone's head will roll. For example, when the Long-Term Capital Management hedge fund collapsed in October

Table 3.3   Extremes of behaviour

Control		
Loose control		*Tight control*
• Process is not generally valued • Flexibility is important • Things tend to emerge – there is little or no defined strategy • Few records are kept • Rules, what rules?		• Processes and procedures are followed to the letter • Innovation is usually limited • Record-keeping tends to be meticulous • Costs are tracked carefully • Breaking rules is frowned upon • Strategy is defined and cascaded throughout the organization

Survival	
Achievement-based	*Tradition/Network-based*
• Focus is on getting the job done to the exclusion of all else • Achievements are well publicized • Challenge is embraced and sought out • Innovation is important • Thought leadership is critical • Speaking out is accepted and expected	• Sponsorship by powerful individuals is essential • Knowledge is openly shared with people • The organization's history is respected • Innovation is rarely rapid • Authority is respected

Risk	
Risk-averse	*Risk-seeking*
• Risks are identified and recorded carefully • Everyone is aware of the risks of taking action • As much information as possible is used to support arguments • Plans are meticulously created • People are unwilling to take spontaneous action	• Focus is on action, not planning • Headline risks only are considered • When things go wrong, the emphasis is on action, not analysis • Failure is acceptable • Innovation is expected

Time	
Time-rich	*Time-poor*
• Immediate results are rare • People do not deliver on time, it's not important to them • Quality is more important than speed • Consensus is important when making decisions • It's OK to spend time talking to people	• Action speaks louder than words • Little time is spent socializing • Fast results are essential • Quick decision making is the norm • Judgement is used wisely • Quality is a low priority

Trust	
High trust	*Low trust*
• Information and views are shared openly • Teamwork is important; loners are not welcome • It's OK to fail, but learn from mistakes • Responsibility is readily accepted	• The political landscape counts • People defend their corners • Evidence is kept to support decisions • A blame culture dominates • People do not share knowledge • Teamwork is rare

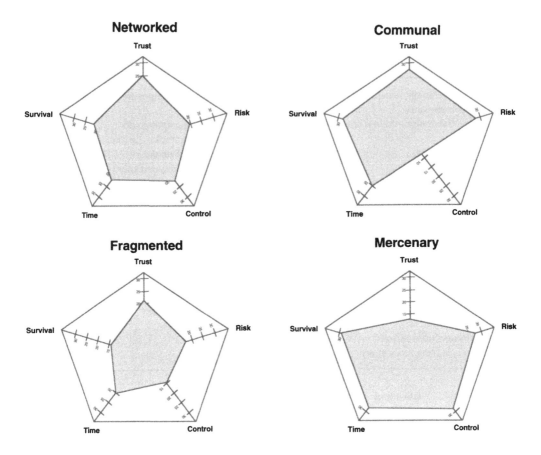

Figure 3.7   Dominant behaviours and culture

1998, the Union Bank of Switzerland lost $700 million. As a result, the chief executive and a number of senior members of the bank were sacked.[13] Communal cultures tend to score highly in all but control. Passion-driven organizations depend on high trust, action orientation and a strong desire to take risks. Focus is on winning, and as a result control is often seen to get in the way of growth and achievement. Networked cultures have a balance about them that the others lack. They can be considered middle-of-the-road organizations: dependable, reliable, unflappable, but unlikely to set the world alight. Risk tends to be viewed as a necessary evil, and when risks are taken these are calculated and usually follow a defined process that often requires a long period of consultation and consideration before action. As a result, time is not considered to be a great issue unless there is pressure from external forces, such as regulators and hostile takeovers. Finally, within fragmented cultures, the behaviours are somewhat muted, mainly because people work very much on their own. People usually only trust themselves to get things done, and survival is typically based on performance only.

As with the culture assessment, the purpose of the behaviour assessment is to get an initial understanding of how to behave within the client organization and understand what people do to get on. Even if this is known at an elementary level, there is less room for error. Furthermore, the focus on dominant behaviours provides the consultant with clues to look out for and hence enable them to bed in more readily with the client. As with the core culture assessment, the results may vary, particularly when a client sits on the boundary of two cultures.

Summary

This chapter has completed the introduction to the concept of cultural intelligence. It has introduced two simple but effective models for assessing a client's culture and dominant behaviours. The next stage is to begin to apply this to the consultancy life cycle to ensure that it moves from the abstract to the practical. This is the purpose of Part II.

II Applying cultural intelligence in consultancy

The issue that all consultancies face is how to win and retain clients. At first glance all that this might require is the ability to sell and deliver high-value consulting. But with discerning clients and an increasingly competitive market place this is too simplistic. As we have seen in Part I, consultants and indeed consultancies that focus purely on intellectual and technical qualities are failing to address the softer elements of the profession that make the client come back for more. Success has more to do with how the consultancy is delivered than what is delivered. Clearly the application of neurolinguistic programming techniques and emotional intelligence can help, but, as we saw in Part I, the essential ingredient is cultural intelligence.

The cultural intelligence model introduced in Chapter 3 helps us to address this, but what we now have to do is to bring it alive within the context of the major consultancy processes. Developing a culturally intelligent approach requires subtle changes to the standard consultancy process along with changes to the way we all behave as professionals. Therefore, cultural intelligence is not designed to introduce yet another consulting model that purports to provide high income or flawless results. Instead it is designed to provide the basis for enhancing the way the consultancy is delivered, irrespective of the model chosen. It is about making consultants more client-centric rather than process- or technique-centric. This allows any firm to enhance its own particular variant of the consulting model, rather than rip it up and start again. This will allow the concept to be more readily accepted and applied more easily.

Part II addresses the changes that should be made to the way consultancy is sold and delivered. It alludes to the changes that we as individual consultants can make to the way we behave and interact with our clients. It does not address firm issues, which will be discussed in Part III. At the end of Part II the consultant will know how to apply their craft within the four cultures.

Part II consists of five chapters:

- Chapter 4 outlines the basic consultancy life cycle and describes where cultural intelligence can be applied.
- Chapter 5 reviews the account management process and outlines how it can be advanced by applying the cultural intelligence concept. It also introduces three account management models (separated, integrated and assimilated) and describes how these can be effectively applied within each of the four cultures to develop account-winning strategies. Finally, it describes what it means to be a culturally intelligent account manager.
- Chapter 6 begins by describing the typical sales cycle in relation to consulting, some of the difficulties experienced by consultants within the sales process and how to overcome them. It introduces some models of selling and enhances these by describing how the sales process can be adjusted to take into account the four cultures. In addressing the sales process in each of the four cultures, the chapter details how to prepare for the sale and where the focus of the sale and should lie, and describes the role of the culturally intelligent salesperson.
- Chapter 7 details the engagement process, which is probably the most important part of the consulting life cycle and where the majority of the client contact takes place. The chapter begins by describing the typical client and firm engagement management processes. It then details how to culturally prepare the engagement team prior to their starting work with the client. It also outlines how the engagement management processes can be adjusted to cater for each culture. As well as providing some practical advice for consultants entering each of the client cultures for the first time, the chapter describes how

projects and programmes should be managed, and how to address politics in each of the four cultures.

- Chapter 8 completes Part II by reviewing the importance of relationship management and how to approach the relationship-building process in each of the four cultures. It starts by looking at the concept of trust and its importance to the relationship-building and indeed the entire consulting process. It then reviews what we currently know about creating effective client relationships. Having addressed this, it describes how relationship management strategies can be created and applied both in a general sense and for each of the four cultures.

4 Cultural intelligence and the consultancy process

Look where you will in the world, consultancy brings great benefits or it creates great mischief. It seldom follows a middle road, but if client and consultant learn to work together effectively, massive added value will come about almost as a matter of course.[1]

There are many different processes for delivering consultancy. And although every consultancy has its own variant and every book provides its own models, they are much the same. Figure 4.1 shows a typical consulting process – by no means extensive, but one which shows the major activities.

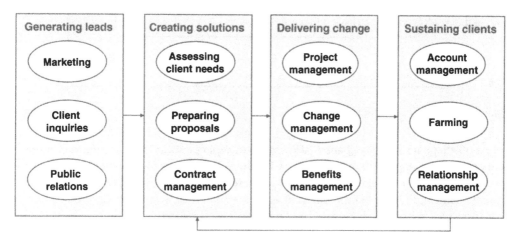

Generating leads	Creating solutions	Delivering change	Sustaining clients
Marketing	Assessing client needs	Project management	Account management
Client inquiries	Preparing proposals	Change management	Farming
Public relations	Contract management	Benefits management	Relationship management

Figure 4.1   The consultancy process

As Figure 4.1 suggests, consultancy can be reducced to a simple process. And like any process, it is not always successful because there are many points of failure. Ultimately, I believe the consulting process boils down to the efficient and effective management of four key and interlocking processes – account management, sales management, engagement management and relationship management (Figure 4.2). Sales management and engagement management lie at the core, as it is here where the consultant spends the most time with their clients. It is also when the client–consultant relationship needs to be at its best. But what does best mean? I believe that in this instance best means demonstrating concern for the client, understanding how it works, and matching this through the way the sale is executed and the engagement delivered. These two core processes can be wrapped up within account management, as this is designed to ensure a continuous stream of fee income is established for the consultancy by farming the account and building on the work undertaken within current engagements. Finally, the process of relationship management encapsulates all others, as each will have a relationship component to it.

Reducing the consulting process to these four processes and hence simplifying the broad

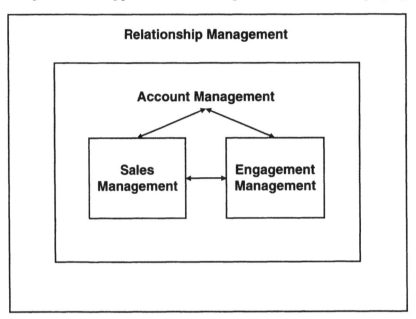

Figure 4.2   The four principal processes

thrust of what consulting is all about allows the concept of cultural intelligence to be applied more effectively. It also allows those firms with their own process to implant the ideas associated with cultural intelligence more easily, as these four processes should be common, even though they might have slightly different names. In addition, consultants should recognize that these processes form the core of their daily activities and hence should be relatively simple to adjust.

The next four chapters outline each of these four processes in more detail. Because the cultural intelligence concept is not designed to replace existing processes, but to enhance them, it is important to introduce the basic tenets of the four main processes before adding the cultural spin to them. Focusing on just the cultural dimension would fail the reader because it would either assume a level of knowledge exists that might be lacking or that every consultancy has identical processes, which of course they do not. I will therefore bring the reader to a common understanding of what each process involves prior to expanding them to take into account the needs of the four cultures.

5 *Account management*

It is well known that consultancies spend a significant amount of time developing strong business relationships with their key clients. The simple reason for this is that it reduces the cost of sales, and produces steady revenue streams. With the maturing and globalizing of the consultancy market, there has been a shift away from small assignments to large single-client engagements.

Account management exists because as much as 70 to 80 per cent of net revenue comes from 20 to 30 per cent of clients. It follows that the consultancy should spend a disproportionate amount of its time getting to know its most profitable clients rather than trying to spend an equal amount of time with all clients. This makes successful relationship and account management even more critical to its business.

In general to be successful at account management, the consultant/partner responsible is usually expected to understand the industry in which the client works (along with the associated tensions, issues and opportunities) as well as how the client's business operates. It also means acting with integrity and honesty, understanding where the account relationship is today, where it might be headed and what factors, changing in what ways, might push the relationship into a more or less productive one. Behaving in ways that are valued by the client cements the relationship and creates a virtuous working environment. Therefore failing to understand the client's culture within the account management process, and acting in a way that is incongruent to it, can lead to a shrinking account. This has important consequences when there are changes within the client and account team. Just because one client accepted the consultancy's offerings, and one account manager was successful, it does not follow that the next client will be as accepting, or the next account manager as successful. A change between account managers rarely covers the cultural issues, and account managers are not necessarily chosen because of their cultural fit with the client. There is, therefore, a strong argument to enhance the handover process to include briefings on client cultures and norms of behaviour.

What is account management?

Account management is a systematic approach to managing how the consultancy sells, delivers and manages its relationships within its high-value clients. It usually involves four major steps:

- Planning the account: this focuses on ensuring that all accounts are strategically aligned and perform to agreed goals and objectives. Planning normally involves targeting new accounts, widening the account once established and managing its decline where necessary.
- Executing the account: this involves establishing and mobilizing the account manage-

ment team, developing the account strategy and assessing the relationship management needs of the account. For the consultancy, this will involve tying account management responsibilities and targets into people's annual objectives, and gaining a detailed understanding of the client, its needs and key decision-makers.

- Managing the account: this is all about ensuring that opportunities and knowledge are shared across the account team and the wider firm where required. In order to manage the account effectively it is necessary to maintain a sales pipeline (see p. 70), measure the value of the work delivered through such things as client satisfaction surveys, and disseminate knowledge and information across the firm about the account and the identified client needs.
- Reporting on the account: because the nature of a client's business will change and the targeting of accounts may shift the firm's attention to other clients, it is essential to report on the account's status. This usually includes assessing it against performance objectives, such as number of opportunities, revenue generated, profitability, cost of sales and so on. This allows the firm to assess the relative importance of its accounts and helps it adjust account strategies where required.

The benefits of account management include:

- Ensuring time and resources are focused on profitable and strategically important clients: this minimizes investment whilst maximizing return.
- Allowing account teams to understand what skills, experience and knowledge the firm needs to bring to the client and hence focus on where it can add the most value: this ensures the account is client- not firm-focused, although there will always be the need to balance the need for fees with the needs of the client. After all, consultancies are there to make money as well as deliver excellent service.
- Managing knowledge and intelligence across the engagement teams working on the client as a way of identifying additional opportunities: this allows the account to have a long-term rather than a short-term focus.

The account management process

Although the typical account management process is quite extensive, the addition of the cultural dimension will help to focus the account team on how to sell and deliver to the client more effectively by tuning them into a client's preferred working style. For the sake of completeness, a typical process with cultural additions has been included here.

PRE-ACCOUNT – TARGETING AND WINNING THE CLIENT

During the initial stages of account development the firm should focus on establishing the routes to market with the potential/new client. In doing so it should attempt to answer the following questions:

- Do we know the client's business strategy?
- Who are the client's competitors and how do they compare to the targeted client?
- What are the client's strengths and weaknesses?

- What is their growth rate?
- Who are the key influencers and what are their roles?

Answering these questions involves assessing the client's current and future business environments, and using this to create a view of potential client needs. Tools such as PEST (political, economic, social and technical) and SWOT (strengths, weaknesses, opportunities and threats) analyses would support this, as will the culture assessment tool of Chapter 3. It would also involve gathering intelligence about the client and its business, using a combination of annual accounts, the Internet and personal contacts. As well as looking at the business environment, the firm would also want to identify key individuals who would need to be targeted and with whom it would wish to strike up a relationship. At the same time it is necessary for the consultancy to assess its own competitive position by establishing the presence of other consultancies, what they are doing and how much value they are adding to the client. In some instances, the consultancy may have had a past relationship with the client, and it may be worth exploring why the consultancy and client relationship faded away. For example, this may have arisen because of poor delivery or a change in personnel. It may have also occurred because of a competitor stealing their client. And we should not forget that it might have resulted from a deliberate move by the consultancy to walk away from the client. Whatever the reason, it is important to understand why the active relationship with the client had been lost.

Once the account has been targeted it is useful to identify those who will become the account team, which, depending on the size of the client, might be a sizeable and potentially global team. Typical roles include the account manager, the service and industry expert, the account planner and a sales director/partner. Having developed an understanding of the client it is then necessary to begin the targeting process by contacting the client and generating the leads for the salespeople. Once an engagement has commenced, the role of the account manager moves into the post-account phase.

POST-ACCOUNT TARGETING – FARMING THE CLIENT

The post-account phase involves continuous dialogue with the client, the engagement team and the salespeople, which for consultancies is usually the engagement team. The purpose here is to enhance the understanding of the client, its business, culture and strategies, as well as develop the account strategy to take the relationship where the consultancy (and client) would like to go. This will involve determining whether an assimilated, integrated or isolated relationship is most appropriate and responding accordingly (see below, 'Getting closer to your clients'). This stage also involves maintaining a record of the client's key decision-makers and influencers: the people who make things happen in the client organization. Because these people are likely to change over time, it is essential that the account manager develops an intelligence network within the client so that they are aware of changes in power and position. This is particularly important within mercenary cultures, where the power will shift from person to person quite frequently. The use of an influence matrix can be useful here (Figure 5.1).

Once the account has been established it is vital to manage the sales pipeline. The purpose of this is to continuously screen the client for new opportunities, assess their value, understand which of the firm's service offerings are appropriate, make proposals to the client, and provide visibility of progress to the wider account team and senior

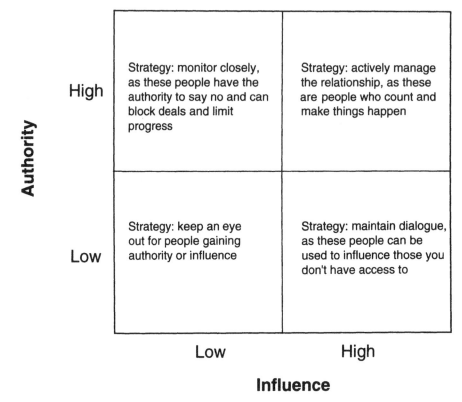

Figure 5.1   Authority and influence

management/partners in the firm. Ultimately, managing the account in this way ensures the consultancy is able to prioritize the offerings it proposes to the client by focusing on those that will add the most value. It also allows the firm to use its resources more effectively. Table 5.1 outlines the definitions that are commonly used in the sales management process.

Table 5.1   The sales pipeline

Status	Definition
Identified	An opportunity within the client has been spotted and a contact has been identified.
Qualified	The opportunity has been discussed with the client and it has decided that it would be worth pursuing.
Abandoned	The opportunity has been discussed with the client and it has decided not to pursue it.
Proposed	Depending on the size and nature of the opportunity, an individual or team will work up a costed proposition or engagement letter. Where required the individual/team will make a presentation to the client to discuss the solution and their credentials. The level of detail required will depend on how trusting the relationship is with the client and on whether the proposal is competitive.
Closed	The client has made its decision to buy the service from the consultancy and is committed to the engagement.
Lost	Having been presented with the proposal, the client has decided not to pursue the solution. This may happen for a variety of reasons and may of course include cultural insensitivity.
Final contract	The contract between the client and consultancy is drawn up and agreed by both parties.
Engagement	The engagement team is mobilized and commences work on the client site.

ACCOUNT DECLINE

Although all consultancies would like to maintain relationships with their clients for years, this is rarely the case. Things are bound to get in the way, such as recessions, changes in senior management, failure to deliver, competitive pressures and so on. In all but those cases where the consultancy has been dismissed by the client, the firm must be prepared to withdraw from the account gracefully. During the process it is necessary to consider whether this is a short-term issue that requires the consultancy to adopt a holding position with the client, or accept that the account is finished and is unlikely to be resurrected in the short term. In the former case, the account manager should maintain an ongoing relationship with the client to ensure that when business picks up, or when there is another opportunity to provide support, they are positioned to win it. Whatever the case, it is essential that this be done in a cost-effective and culturally sensitive way.

Getting closer to your clients

When assessing the cultural dynamic of account management, it is worth considering the work of Berry and his model of acculturation[1] (which I have updated for consultancy). This suggests that when two cultures come together, three outcomes are possible.

- Assimilation: this exists where the consultancy has a perfect fit with the client's culture, so much so that they are perceived as being part of the furniture. In such instances the relationship between the client and consultancy is so strong that the client will feed them new work without the consultants' having to hunt for or farm it. This is any consultancy's dream because it normally negates the need to produce lengthy proposal documents and, of course, reduces the cost of sales. A good example of this is how Bain managed to forge deep relationships with organizations such as National Steel and Chrysler Motors by 'anchoring themselves to the stomach of the business'. In this way they were not only able to increase revenues by 40 to 50 per cent per year between 1973 and the mid-1980s, but also create relationships where their clients would call on them, rather than the other way around.[2]
- Integration (Figure 5.2): here the consultancy displays a sensitivity to the client's culture (because it has a basic understanding of it) and demonstrates this through the way in which it sells and delivers its work. In this case, however, a large degree of independence from the client is maintained, and indeed may be valued by the client because the consultant is able to bring new ideas from other organizations and assignments into its environment. The integrated model came through strongly in a number of the interviews I conducted during the research for this book. For example, in winning work with a major insurance provider in the United Kingdom, one consultant stated that the client had openly mentioned that the reason for choosing them was based on cultural fit. The client stated that the consultancy's culture demonstrated synergy with its own, whilst at the same time bringing other dimensions that would

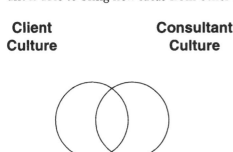

Client Culture   **Consultant Culture**

Figure 5.2   The integrated relationship

challenge their mode of working. The client also stated that it had rejected one consultancy for having a culture that was too similar to its own. This suggests that the assimilation variant is not always the best model to adopt for all clients, and is certainly not always feasible at the time of the sale. Interestingly, when asked whether they had deliberately assessed the client's culture prior to making the sales presentation, the consultant stated they had not – it was the client who raised it. The fact that the client is selecting on cultural fit should be of interest to consultancies. This would mean that cultural fit is likely to be amongst the usual criteria used by clients to select their consultants. Others include past relationships, successful past performance on similar engagements, understanding of the client's business, project management competence, technical credibility and price.[3] I would, however, regard culture as an unwritten criterion, and one that is usually hidden from view. Yet, so often it is the fit between client and consultant that secures the sale. Culture is often the overriding factor.

- Isolation (Figure 5.3): in this instance the client and service provider have nothing in common from a cultural perspective. Selling is based upon technical fit rather than cultural fit. There is nothing wrong with having no commonality in culture, as sometimes the client will need to bring in a team that will shake it up and aggressively drive through change. In other words there are those clients who actually prefer to have consultancy 'done' to them. They are, however, extremely rare, and this type of situation only occurs when there is a crisis that has to be dealt with. At times like this, making it an enjoyable process is of little or no concern to either client or consultant. The real danger with the separated model is that the account is unlikely to flourish beyond the immediate engagement. For example, in a major assignment with an investment bank, the business was sold on the service provider's competency at running large, complex programmes. Because the investment bank lacked these skills, it was less concerned about the consultancy's investment banking experience, and more with its capability at delivering large programmes. In addition, from a cultural perspective, the consultancy was very different, and hence separate, from the investment bank (the bank was mercenary, and the consultancy team was principally networked). The degree of cultural separation was evident at the end of the programme, when apart from a small number of other assignments that required programme management expertise it became almost impossible to sell additional work. However, a core team amongst the engagement team managed to move through the model from isolated to integrated, and as a result was the last to leave. This of course should not be confused with 'going native', which is always a danger for consultants on long-term assignments (see Chapter 10).

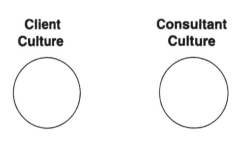

Client Culture　　　　**Consultant Culture**

Figure 5.3　The isolated relationship

Account management strategies in the four cultures

Sophisticated account management processes already exist within the major consultancies, and usually include such steps as client qualification, relationship development, intelligence gathering and so on. Adding a cultural dimension adds real value in two ways.

The first involves designing the account strategy by linking the culture type (mercenary, networked, communal and fragmented) to the degree of acculturation necessary to penetrate the client (assimilation, integration, isolation) as described below:

- Mercenary cultures: the nature of mercenary organizations suggests that assimilation would be the most suitable strategy to aim for. The reason for this is quite simple: get to where the real power is, identify with it, and make yourself indispensable by enhancing the power base through excellent delivery. Maintaining this relationship and position within the organization will take some skill, and it will be necessary to gradually move to other power-brokers as the balance of power changes within the client. Success in the mercenary culture would require aligning the consultancy to one or two powerful individuals.
- Communal cultures: the assimilation variant is also applicable within communal organizations but for different reasons. Because success in the communal culture requires that the individual lives the credo, it would be essential for the account manager to share the passion and take an in-depth interest in the client and what it is trying to achieve. In this way the opportunity to develop a long-term relationship will be greatly enhanced. Unlike in the mercenary culture, the key to success would be to align the consultancy to the whole organization and almost become one with the client, in essence developing a sense of 'we're in this together', so that the client believes the consultancy is there for the long haul.
- Networked cultures: in this case the integration variant is the most appropriate because relationships have to be developed across the whole organization. Thus being able to display a general degree of cultural understanding across all functions would be important. In this way the consultancy would be accepted in every function rather than in just one or two. This would mean, however, having a larger account team, and ensuring each relationship manager within the team was aligned to a particular function.
- Fragmented cultures: here the isolated variant is appropriate, as work will typically be transactional in nature. With the difficulty in getting time in people's diaries and the generally isolated nature of the organization's activity, the account team would have to work with individuals rather than groups. They would also have to recognize that once an assignment was complete, it might be necessary to move elsewhere within the organization to find the next one. When compared to the other three cultures, this is the hardest to manage and the most difficult to farm unless you can develop a deep relationship with a key function or operating division.

The second area where the account management process could be enhanced is within the management of accounts over time. In this case Berry's model can be used to assess where the relationship currently is, and where it should be. Many factors apart from culture would have to be taken into account in this process, including current revenue streams, future revenue potential, whether the client is a potential key account, the general performance of the client organization, the performance of the sector within which it sits and so on. If, for example, an account has the potential of becoming a cash cow, and the current assessment of cultural fit is isolated, the consultancy may invest heavily to become more integrated or assimilated with the clients. Equally, if the revenue is dwindling, the consultancy may take deliberate steps to move itself from an assimilated to a networked or isolated position. The key point to this is that, just as cultural congruence can cement a relationship, cultural incongruence can be used to break it. The process through which relationships with a client can be gradually severed by the service provider can be difficult, especially as the client may feel dependent upon it. Using culture as a way of gently letting a client go could benefit the situation where the consultancy (or client) has outstayed its welcome. And hopefully this can be achieved without upsetting the client (well, not too much). The other advantage of letting clients go gently is that they are more likely to leave the door open for future opportunities. Ultimately, it is about adding value, and all clients approve of consultancies that are willing to hold up their hands when they are not doing so. It is a shame that so many consultancies fail to do this, instead favouring to act as leeches and continue to extract fees until they are invited to leave.

Assessing accounts by culture

The best way to start addressing the cultural fit of the consultancy is to make an assessment of existing and future accounts. This would involve the following steps.

1. Assess the culture of each account using the basic culture questionnaire provided in Chapter 3. The best way to do this is to have account managers fill in the questionnaire for each of their clients. Alternatively, they could make a rough-and-ready assessment based upon their experience of the client to date.
2. Identify all work that has been won and lost within each client culture. This should make the distinction between that work that has been lost because of competition and that which has been abandoned for other reasons (such as lack of budget, change of strategy and so on). This allows the firm to make the distinction between work that may have been lost because of poor cultural fit (the work that has been lost to one of the consultancy's competitors) and that which may have been lost because of poor definition of client need (work that has been abandoned). Each would require a different response from the account manager.
3. Identify key accounts (new and existing) and assess client culture, as in step 1 above.
4. Plot the results onto the culture model (see Figure 5.4 for an example).

Once plotted, the results will indicate a number of things.

- A clear grouping for winning work (for example in the networked culture of Figure 5.4) would suggest the consultancy has a natural bias toward one of the four cultures. The notion of 'like attracts like' is relevant here, as the consultancy will typically seek out and win the majority of its work within a culture that matches its own or in one it feels the most comfortable with. Considering that consultancies based upon the partnership model have a tendency toward the networked culture, it would be unsurprising to see this type of pattern. From an account management perspective, this can be addressed in one of two ways. First, more attention could be paid to those cultures where less work is won by targeting clients that fall into the other three cultures (see Figure 3.4 for examples). Second, the consultancy could build on its success by making this natural bias more specific by seeking to enhance it. This could be achieved by using the techniques and information introduced in this book. With little to differentiate itself from its competition, the consultancy could use this cultural bias to its advantage.
- Depending on the groupings, work lost in a competitive situation would suggest a number

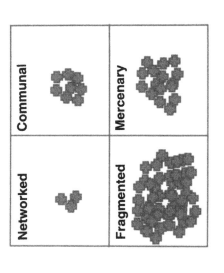

Win

Loss (to competition)

Loss (client does not buy)

Target

Figure 5.4 Plotting account outcome by culture

of things. If, for example, a lot of work was lost in the dominant sales culture it would indicate that the firm doesn't actually know why it is either winning or losing work in this or indeed any other culture. It will probably put it down to price or technical fit, when it might just be due to another consultancy having a better cultural fit with their targeted client. It might also be because they hadn't taken the trouble to refine the sales style to fit the client's particular biases (see next chapter). If work is being lost in the non-dominant cultures this would suggest that the consultancy is not adjusting its style to other client cultures. This may of course be due to the consultancy adopting a single formulaic approach to selling its services.

- When assessing why work has been abandoned a few points are worth stating. This type of sales result usually occurs when the consultancy either has an existing relationship with a client and is suggesting new projects which the client is not interested in, or where the client is new and the consultant is involved with post-sale negotiations. In both cases the reasons for the loss are more wide-ranging than those in the competitive situation and include the inability to close the sale, poor targeting of service offerings, and the client changing its mind. It may also reflect a cooling of the client–consultant relationship. It is important to assess the reasons why the work has gone away, as this will have a bearing on the way the account should be managed, especially if it is due to a cooling off of the relationship. Ideally this should take place immediately after the client decision. The use of an after-action review would be one way to achieve immediate feedback.[4] The United States Army uses the after-action review as a means of continuous learning and improvement. It originated during the Vietnam War, where the soldiers in the field knew more than those at headquarters. The review allows people to learn immediately after an event, irrespective of whether it was a success or failure. The key thing is that it takes place immediately. Conducting an after-action review usually takes between 20 and 30 minutes, and should answer the following questions:
  - What should have happened?
  - What actually happened?
  - What were the differences between what should have and what actually happened?
  - What lessons can be drawn from the experience, and how can any strengths revealed be built upon and any weaknesses reduced or eliminated?
- When reviewing the pattern of targeted clients, any bias should be immediately obvious. The targeted clients should be compared to the wins and losses in each culture, as this will identify wider issues associated with the way the consultancy deals with particular cultures. For example, in Figure 5.4 the consultancy has targeted a number of mercenary clients, even though it wins very little work in mercenary cultures (as demonstrated by the few wins and myriad losses). This will clearly present issues when it comes to securing work from these targeted clients. And without updating the sales process to reflect the particular needs of the mercenary culture, it is unlikely to be successful.

There are clear benefits in conducting such an exercise because it forces the account manager and the firm to consider how it currently targets its clients, prepares its sales pitches and manages accounts once established.

The culturally intelligent account manager

Enhancing the account management process to make it more culturally intelligent requires the consultancy to do the following for each of its clients. First, it should perform the account assessment process described above to understand how successful it is at selling in each of the four cultures. Next, it needs to update its processes by incorporating a cultural assessment as part of its account targeting process. It will also need to consider just how close, from a cultural perspective, it wishes to be to its clients. This would involve considering whether an assimilated, integrated or isolated relationship is called for. Third, it should develop culturally intelligent account managers. This can be achieved through training, or by tapping into those consultants who show cultural sensitivity. However, most firms seem to allocate account managers randomly. As a result, many accounts wither on the vine rather than thrive because the client and account manager do not click. The culturally intelligent account manager would take more trouble to understand their client's culture so that they are able to understand what it means for selling and delivering their services and how to manage the client–consultant relationship. There would be, for example, no harm in sitting down with the client (potential or existing) and completing the culture questionnaire. Not only will this be of interest to the client but it also demonstrates the concern the firm places on making the relationship work. The account manager should also ensure that their sales and engagement teams are suitably prepared for selling into and working with their client. This will involve providing briefs that should describe the preferred working style of the client and how salespeople and consultants should adjust their behaviours when interacting with them. This final point is very important, because successful account management depends on both the sales and delivery process. And, if cultural intelligence is to work, then these two processes have to be updated to incorporate culture (see Chapter 6 for how the sales process can be enhanced, and Chapter 7 for the delivery processes).

THE CULTURALLY INTELLIGENT ACCOUNT MANAGER

- understands the basic cultural differences of the four client cultures
- will demonstrate client sensitivity by seeking client input into understanding its culture and preferred working style
- will take time to prepare their sales and engagement teams so that they are able to match the sales and delivery styles to the client culture
- will match the relationship strategy required for each culture (see Chapter 8)
- will focus their services according to the client's preferred working style.

Summary

It is very tempting to think that account management is just farming a client for additional fees, or about wining and dining the client and using this as a means of selling new work. It is neither. Interestingly, many clients hate to be thought of as being a consultancy's next meal, can't abide consultants who are failing to add value and certainly do not like arrogant firms that impose solutions and change on them without considering them as unique. Moreover, many clients often perceive wining and dining as a subtle approach to the hard sell and do not believe them to be sincere relationship-building activities. The best way to add value is to take the trouble to understand more about the client and the way it works, and use this to match the sales and delivery processes to its preferred working style based on its culture.

6 Sales and sales management

Most advisors are a little uncomfortable with overt selling. They would like to believe that the quality of their work speaks for itself, that the need for their services is self-evident to the client and that it is therefore unnecessary to belabour the obvious in selling. Alas this is not always true.[1]

Selling services is different from selling products. Whereas products usually have an underlying intrinsic value and utility to them, a service's value is less well defined, involves much more human contact and very often requires a skilled professional to deliver it. This distinction also exists in law, where separate acts apply to the delivery of products and services. For example, an artist who paints your portrait is classed as supplying a service because it is based on their expertise and skill. Buying a suit from a tailor, however, is classed as supplying goods because the customer is paying for the suit, and not the tailor's expertise.[2] If we accept that the delivery of services involves the selling of expertise, we can argue that it is far more focused on individual or group capability than product capability. Selling consultancy falls into this service category and for a number of reasons is very different from, and much harder than, selling products:[3]

- Because consultants are required to sell themselves (and ultimately their firm) success in the sales process depends on creating trust between themselves and the client. This has to be done very quickly because a sale can be won or lost within the first few minutes of the presentation, and in some cases before the presentation starts.
- Buying decisions are rarely taken lightly within client organizations because of the business-critical nature of the decision. Indeed, the very fact that consultants are being invited to help the client suggests there is a difficult problem to resolve.
- It is critical that the consultants assess the type of relationship the client wants, as getting this wrong can also present problems at the time of the sale. On the whole most clients expect a long-term relationship and commitment from the consultancy. Unfortunately, this is often at odds with some firms because of their short-term and transactional focus, and can create major tensions in certain organizations. Of course there are also clients that prefer short-term engagements using the consultancy to resolve a very specific issue. Knowing which you are dealing with is important.
- Consultants do not perceive themselves as salespeople. They may hate the sales situation, feel like failures if they lose the sale and dislike feedback when they get it. That said, it is important to be able to roll with the punches and accept any critiques as a learning experience.
- Consultants also have to deliver engagements, and if the sales team is different from the delivery team it can create confusion. For example, the client may be unsure of exactly whom it is buying and the delivery team may experience problems understanding and delivering what has been sold. There is therefore some merit in having the team who will

be delivering the work present at the sales meeting even if they are not involved with the sales presentation itself. This avoids one of the major issues about selling consultancy. All too often a senior member of the firm makes the sale and the client never sees that person again, but instead sees plenty of junior or inexperienced consultants. Selling with the A team and delivering with the B team is unacceptable.

Of all the issues identified above it is the consultant's reluctance to sell that is the most significant, and this needs to be addressed before we can turn to the cultural dimension to selling.

Why consultants find it difficult to sell

Consultants are not natural salespeople. The training they receive and the experience they amass is primarily focused on enhancing and building on their technical ability. They are strong problem solvers who pride themselves on being right. Indeed, the culture and operating principles of the firms in which they work means that failure is rarely tolerated, so it is important for the consultants to continuously demonstrate success. Sales is basically a numbers game, in which sales are won and deals are lost. Professional salespeople know this and have become adept at developing new leads and closing deals. As I mentioned above, consultants therefore feel uncomfortable with selling because it exposes them to the possibility of failure. They also dislike selling because of its poor image. Sales is often portrayed as a greaseball's job that requires underhand tactics, little knowledge about what you are selling and a silver tongue. This is something that sits uneasily with the professional integrity of the consultant. Unfortunately, as the consultant gains seniority within a firm the focus on doing becomes less pronounced, whilst the need to sell and demonstrate sales capability becomes more important. This is why so many consultants end up leaving the profession and moving back into industry.

Helping the consultant sell

There are many publications, books and training events dedicated to making successful salespeople, sales teams, and gaining and retaining of customers. In the last few years this general advice has been augmented by NLP[4] techniques that are designed to improve the level of rapport between the salesman and the purchaser by using the subconscious and automatic responses that are ingrained in the workings of the human brain. It is believed that this makes the sale of the product or service much easier (see Chapter 1 for more details on NLP). However, the individualistic perspective of NLP in itself does not help in the sale of services to the wider organizational audience. For example, many sales situations involve presentations to groups, or the production of documents that outline the key elements of the service to be delivered. These often fail to win the sale and the reasons for this are often couched in hard phrases, such as 'you're too expensive' or 'I didn't like the technical details' and so on. But considering that consultancies often sell ostensibly the same products and services, price and technical fit are not sufficient to explain the lost sale in all but a few cases. I believe culture counts and it is essential that consultancies develop a basic understanding of the culture into which they are selling before they make their sales pitch.

The preference of problem solving over selling creates issues during the sales process, especially when exploring client needs and closing the sale. It is this first point that is a particular issue because consultants tend to jump to solutions too quickly during the sales process and make assumptions about what the client needs. This means that the full extent of a client problem is rarely uncovered. For the client this means that its needs are not fully understood, and for the consultant, the chance of a reduced scope (and hence fee) is all the more likely. Fortunately, there have been a number of models that can help the consultant navigate through the painful process of selling. For completeness, an outline of the most useful has been included here.

Any sale involves the following five steps:[5]

- Recognition of needs: the client has to recognize that it has a problem or opportunity that requires outside help. Organizations only buy when they are dissatisfied with their current situation. This may arise from upside as well as downside issues – for example, cutting costs, improving market share, merging or acquiring another company, delivering a complex project and so on. All create the necessary level of dissatisfaction that can lead to the need to engage consultants. The role of the consultant in this instance is to explore the client's current situation and determine where any issues exist. With an existing client this role would fall to the account manager and the engagement team.
- Evaluation of options: once the consultant has established the need, the next thing the client must do is to determine how and from whom it will buy. Depending on the scale and complexity of the requirement, the client may prefer to make the process competitive between a number of suppliers. Or if it has established a trusted relationship with a single supplier it may ask for its help without approaching any others. In either case the role of the consultant is to explore the synergies between their service and the client's needs. It is here where the cultural sensitivity can help, as the consultant will be able to focus on those elements of their service that match the client's preferred style. In addition, understanding the likely buying and intervention styles will ensure the service offering is expressed in a way that is more likely to meet client expectations (see later).
- Resolution of concerns: where the sale is associated with a complex problem or proposed solution it will probably raise a number of issues and concerns which must be resolved prior to the sale's closure. Such concerns if not suitably addressed can result in the consultant losing the sale. The biggest issue facing consultancies is that the sale is rarely simple because the nature of the client's problems dictates a complex solution. That said, there are occasions when the client will be body shopping for specific skills or known solutions. This is especially true of mercenary and fragmented cultures.
- Purchase: once the deal has been done, the role of the consultant is to make the remainder of the sales process run as quickly and as smoothly as possible. Letters of engagement, contracts and mobilizing the engagement team are vital elements of the consultancy sales process. In large sales, because the bid team would have lived and breathed the client for days if not weeks, it is usual to find the same people forming the core of the engagement team. Where the sale is small or medium scale, it is likely that the bid team will have to be augmented by other consulting staff.
- Implementation: a sale is never completed until the engagement has delivered and met the expectations that were set at the time of the sale. Executing consulting assignments is rarely a straightforward affair and the implementation stage of the engagement can be particularly fraught, as we saw with Westpac (Chapter 3).

A technique known as SPIN® selling is particularly relevant to the consultant as it leads them through the process of selling (above) and helps them to spend more time exploring issues and identifying needs than jumping to solutions.[6] The technique was based upon a 12-year research programme that studied 35,000 sales calls. The research concluded that successful sales depended on asking questions, not telling the client about functions or capabilities. It also found that most salespeople tell more than they ask, even though they know that it should be the other way around. The SPIN® method is designed to force the salesperson to ask more questions in order to uncover the real client need. The acronym stands for situation, problem, implication and need.

- *Situation*: it is important for the consultant to begin the sales meeting by establishing the current situation of the organization. Any consultant worth their salt would have already picked up some key information about the client from the Internet, previous projects and any contact they or their colleagues might have had with the client in the past. The types of question that would be required at this stage of the meeting include:
  - What is the company's turnover and profit?
  - How many people work in IT?
  - What system do you use for management accounting?
  The purpose of situation questions is to establish some general facts about the client and to demonstrate that you understand them. It is important not to ask too few or too many. Too few and it will be unlikely that you will uncover any problem areas. Ask too many and the client may become impatient.
- *Problem*: having established the current situation, the consultant should then explore the client's problems. Such problems will not necessarily be associated with difficulties the organization is having, as they could be associated with positive growth plans or opportunities the client wishes to pursue. The consultant should attempt to identify as many issues and concerns as possible, as this will allow a fuller picture of client need to be developed. It is here where the consultant is most at risk from jumping into solution mode. Problem questions are designed to uncover what are known as implied needs that can then be further explored through the implication questions. Typical problem questions might be:
  - Are you happy with your existing accounting processes and systems?
  - Is your IT department providing you with value for money?
  - Are you satisfied with the levels of service from your suppliers?
- *Implication*: the idea behind this additional exploration is to establish the scale and criticality of the client's problems or opportunities. Understanding the implications of these questions in terms of numbers of people affected, financial impacts and so on will develop a much broader and deeper knowledge of the problem and what solution might be appropriate. This also allows the sales meeting to be more productive. Questions that would be appropriate during this stage would include:
  - What are the consequences of *x*?
  - How many people/functions are affected?
  - What would the financial implications of *y* be?
- *Need*: it is through the combination of smart questioning around the problem area and its implications that surface the real, rather than perceived, client needs. At this stage the consultant can highlight what options might be open to the client in solving its problems and pinpointing what the consultancy can offer. Within SPIN® this is known as the need pay-off questions. Examples include:

- If you were able to solve this problem what benefits might you derive?
- Why is it important for you to solve this problem?

These questions help identify the benefits and solutions the client might buy and allow the consultant to begin matching the offering to the need.

Two sales life cycles

There are two forms of selling, hunting and farming. The former involves selling into a client for the first time and requires the consultancy to target those clients they would like to work with, develop an account strategy, and craft appropriate propositions that can be shared with the client. The process of selling in this instance follows some standard steps, including prospecting, cold calling, conducting meetings with the client's decision-makers and making proposals (that is, following the SPIN® model). Once a proposal has been accepted and the consultants are on site, the sales life cycle shifts to farming (Figure 6.1). This kicks in

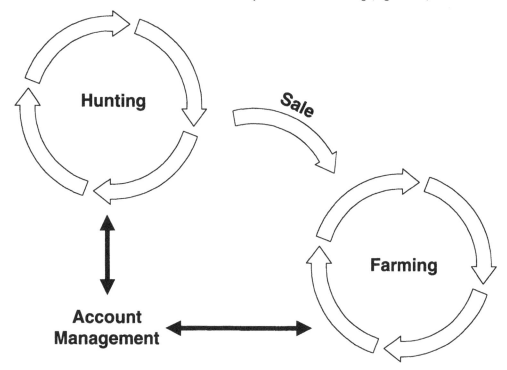

Figure 6.1   The two sales life cycles

after the consultancy has established its reputation for delivery and has won the trust of the client. Farming involves developing relationships across the client, identifying opportunities, feeding these back to the account manager and making new proposals. The proposals in this instance are unlikely to be competitive, which makes the process of selling a much easier and less costly exercise. Of course there is no room for complacency, as the consultancy will still need to produce quality proposals and maintain its reputation for delivery. It must also continue to advance its understanding of the client and its culture.

Selling modes

Although SPIN® is capable of leading the consultant through the sales process, success also depends on matching the selling mode to the customer buying mode. Three modes of selling exist:[7]

- *Transaction selling* (the intrinsic value buyer) in which the buyer treats the supplier as a commodity and is mainly, or only, interested in price and convenience. In transactional sales, buyers have a clear view of what they want, and are not interested in exploring the problem. In this instance they tend to body shop with their suppliers. This means that they are interested in buying either a specific product or skill set, such as project management, rather than a service. Transactional sales tend to be highly competitive, with a number of suppliers vying for the client's business. In this instance price will probably be the overriding selection criterion, which may force the top-tier consultancy out of the market (unless it is willing to make substantial discounts). The consultant should make the purchase as painless and convenient as possible by focusing on the basic client need. There may be little value in exploring the wider needs, as the client will perceive its problem in a very narrow way.
- *Consultative selling* (the extrinsic value buyer) in which buyers demand and are willing to pay for a sales effort that creates new value and benefits beyond the basic transaction. Unlike the transactional sale, the client typically does not have a clear understanding of the problem it is trying to resolve. The consultancy can help the client by exploring the extent of the problem and providing additional insights based upon its experience. In this case the consultancy should focus on needs analysis, as this is where the most value can be added.
- *Enterprise selling* (the strategic value buyer) in which buyers demand an extraordinary level of value creation from a key supplier. This type of selling is most appropriate for the larger consultancies, such as the Big Five, because the client will expect to leverage the combined knowledge of the firm. Clients that are strategic buyers usually expect the consultancy to become actively involved with projects across most, if not all, of their functions. Success therefore depends upon aligning the client's and consultancy's strategic interests. In essence it is about creating a long-term relationship that is predicated on a shared journey and commitment. Therefore the process of selling would begin at the strategic level and involve the consultancy developing a shared vision of the future with the client, and then working with it to realize it.

David Maister,[8] who has written much about the professional firm, adds to this by considering both the degree of customization necessary to solve the client's problems and the degree of client contact required during the delivery of the service. He classifies clients as either seeking:

- Pharmacists – where they are buying a familiar service with little counselling, consultation or contact. In such cases the client will expect the service to be delivered according to strict standards at minimum cost. The type of service being sold is typically commoditized and would be offered by most consultancies. Moreover, when it comes to the engagement it is likely that it will be executed by junior and/or inexperienced consultants who will follow the consultancy's standard methodologies and procedures. The use of junior consultants will keep costs down. It is unlikely that the client would expect to see, or be willing to pay for, experienced consultants on this type of assignment. The client is uninterested in innovation, and more concerned about guaranteeing quick (and cheap) results.

- Nurses – where they are buying a relatively familiar service, but require guidance during its delivery. In this case the client still expects a commoditized service, but with more interaction. It is unwilling to leave the consultants to work in the background and only surface once the job is done. Here visibility is important, and it is essential that the client feels involved throughout the whole process. Because of this, the consultancy would opt for a mix of junior and/or inexperienced consultants to perform the work along with a small number of more seasoned consultants, who would manage the client and guide it through the process.
- Brain surgeons – where clients are buying high levels of customization, creativity and innovation, and want to be left out of the process. Clients who are in this mode of buying will not be selecting on price as they recognize that solving their complex problem will not be easy. As clients they will expect the consultancy to provide subject-matter experts and experienced consultants. They will not take too kindly to be being swamped with junior consultants with little or no commercial or consulting experience. The essential ingredient to being able to convince the client of the consultant's ability to deliver will be the application of the firm-wide experience and expertise: creativity is king for this buying mode.
- Psychotherapists – where clients are buying a high level of customization, creativity and innovation and want to be intimately involved with the process. As with the brain surgeon, this buying mode requires the consultancy to bring its experience and expertise to bear on the client problem rather than the rank and file of junior consultants. But in this instance client involvement is vital, as it will want to understand the problem and be involved in both generating and executing the solution. As a result the engagement will become a shared journey between the client and consultant. Success will require strong relationship management skills, and will probably require the consultancy to deploy very senior consultants and possibly partners.

Combining the three selling modes and the four client types would suggest that pharmacists and perhaps nurses would suit the transactional sales mode, brain surgeons would suit consultative selling and psychotherapists would suit enterprise selling. Misreading the preferred intervention approach of the client can have disastrous results. For example, Maister discusses a situation in which a client wanted to improve its marketing success. However, instead of seeking a permanent fix, the client wanted a quick-fix solution that would cause the least disruption to its business. No matter how hard the consultancy tried to sell in the long-term approach, the client wanted none of it, and the consultancy lost the business.

The cultural dimension to the sales process

Just as it is important to understand the client's preferred intervention style and buying behaviour, it is critical to recognize that the client's culture will have an impact on how they buy, and on the selling approach that should be adopted by the consultancy.

MERCENARY

Within mercenary cultures, the sales focus should be on the benefits and timings of the engagement rather than the process. This is because mercenary cultures are action-orientated and generally care little for the process through which the work will be delivered. Although process is important and may have to be explored during the sales meeting/presentation, it is necessary to keep this type of information in the background. Therefore when preparing the sales presentation it is a good idea to flip the material around so that it begins with the outcomes, benefits, timings and capabilities rather than describing the background of the meeting. Mercenary organizations will look for confidence in the consultancy's ability to deliver the service, so it is important to have a strong consultant making the pitch. They will also look for a deep understanding of their organization and in some cases expect the consultancy to be highly creative (the brain surgeon mode). What they won't want is to get deeply involved with the change, as they have their daily business to manage. This has implications for the engagement, as we will see in Chapter 7. In terms of the preferred buying style, mercenary organizations tend to opt for the transactional mode, rather than anything else, as they will believe themselves to be in control of their organization and fully understand what they need from the consultants and the engagement. One of the other factors involved with selling to mercenary cultures is the identification of the power base. Knowing who holds the buy decision is essential, and it is usually one person. Seeking them out and convincing them that you are capable of delivering what they need when they need it is vital. A decision is normally given at the sales meeting, or very shortly after.

NETWORKED

Networked organizations need to understand what the changes will mean for the way they work and for their employees. The process of change is therefore far more important than the benefits. Of course benefits must still be a factor, but unlike the mercenary organization, they are not the overriding factor. Sales meetings and presentations will need to focus on gaining consensus, and it will be necessary to spend time prior to the sales event gaining support from the client's decision-makers and stakeholders. Because networked organizations are less arrogant than mercenary cultures, they are more willing to explore the dimensions of the change, as they will want to understand how it will be implemented. This means that the sales presentation must allow sufficient time for discussion and agreement. With respect to deciding on whether to purchase the service, the networked culture will take its time, and it is unlikely to decide at the meeting. Indeed, there may be a number of additional questions that have to be resolved prior to the final agreement being made. The networked culture will also look for the risks and will expect the consultancy's reassurance that they will be appropriately managed throughout the engagement.

FRAGMENTED

Within fragmented organizations, the sales strategy should focus on individuals, as it is rare that the organization will buy corporately. This provides the consultancy with ample opportunity to secure work across the whole organization by seeking out needs on an individual or functional basis. Recognizing that the fragmented organization can be considered to be a collection of individuals, it is essential that the salesperson concentrate on how the engagement can improve the position/situation of the person they are selling to rather than the organization as a whole. This means focusing on what the individual and local needs are, and then designing an appropriate solution. Decision-making at a local level will be fast, and the consultancy should expect a rapid close to the sale (either positively or negatively) followed by a fast mobilization of the engagement team. The real advantage of selling into the fragmented culture is the opportunity to make multiple and potentially simultaneous sales across the client. Because of this it is often a good idea to have more than one salesperson working on the account. A word of warning: although it is best to sell to individuals within the fragmented organization, there will be occasions when the sales team will be making a pitch to a group. The problem here is that unless the team can have access to the individual client representatives before the sales presentation, they could be in for a rough ride as the client representatives may fight amongst themselves and play the consultants off against their colleagues. So although the client will be there as a single group, individuals will be fiercely protecting their own patch. Unfortunately in this instance it will be impossible to please everyone. However, if the sales team can gain access to the client before the sales meeting they ought to be able to tailor the presentation so that each person present can be seen to be getting something out of the proposition.

COMMUNAL

The communal organization requires long-term commitment from the consultancy, and will not be interested in working with a firm that is not prepared to be with them for an extended period. Once a communal organization trusts the consultancy, it will want it to take on a trusted advisor role. Because it is a combination of both the networked and mercenary cultures it will be interested in the benefits of the consultancy engagement as well as the effects it will have on the organization and its people. The sales presentation should therefore cover benefits, process, impacts and shared commitment. Of these, it is the shared commitment that is the most important. Displaying a real belief, in what the client wants to achieve and showing how the consultancy is capable of stepping up to their mark is essential. In essence, if you believe, the client will believe. Communal cultures will not seek out risks and concerns during the sales meeting, as they will wish to focus on making it happen (whatever it is). Consultants who focus on the risks during the presentation will be perceived by the client as risk-averse, and not willing to rise to the challenge and commit to the change. Clearly risks will be present, but these have to be addressed during the engagement and should be described in the sales presentation as obstacles that have to be overcome. As with the networked organization, the communal organization will want to know what the change will mean for its staff. Therefore, it is important to describe how the staff will be brought along with the change, and ideally they should be involved as much as possible and not have the consultancy imposed upon them. With respect to the timing of the decision this could fall either way. It could be fast or slow and very much depends on the sales pitch and whether it addresses all of the client concerns.

Table 6.1 summarizes the key points that should be borne in mind by the salesperson preparing for sales meetings and presentations.

Summary

Consultants have the difficult job of selling as well as delivering their service. This makes them very different from pure salespeople who are trained to identify needs, buying signs

Table 6.1   Sales focus by culture

Networked	Communal	Mercenary	Fragmented
• Focus on the process and be prepared to discuss how it will work • Make time for discussion • Allow everyone to make their opinion known • Work with the client to generate a shared understanding of the service that is to be provided • Demonstrate patience during the process • Recognize the decision is unlikely to be immediate • Methodologies count, so emphasize them.	• Believe in what you say, and believe it for the client • Demonstrate your commitment to making it happen • Be passionate; if you believe, they will believe • Demonstrate that you are willing to take an active part in their journey • Make it clear what the impact will be on their staff.	• Cut to the chase: what are the benefits of the service? • Don't spend too much time on the why or the how, focus on the when • Emphasize how the service will provide competitive advantage and take out the competition • Keep it brief and to the point • Keep it simple, they do not need to know the complexities • Display confidence in what you say.	• Emphasize how the service will make the client the best in its field • Demonstrate that you're best in your field • Back up your claims with evidence • De-emphasize the need for client teams – these organizations do not value teamwork • Tailor solutions to suit individual or functional need.

THE CULTURALLY INTELLIGENT SALESPERSON

- understands the basic cultural differences of the four client cultures
- focuses on and emphasizes the primary concerns of the culture during preliminary discussions
- tailors the sales material, presentations and selling approach to match the buying needs of the culture
- works with the account manager and engagement manager to prepare the engagement team prior to starting work with the client.

---

and how to close. Consultants on the other hand are trained to consult, problem solve, and identify and deliver solutions. They are consultants first and salespeople second. This makes most feel uncomfortable in the sales situation. It also makes the sales process seem an impossible thing to master as it exposes consultants to their greatest fear, failure. Unfortunately, the ability to sell is an increasingly important skill within consultancy. To improve the likelihood of success it is important to understand how clients will buy, especially in relation to culture. Consultants also need to recognize that selling is a numbers game, where you can't win all of the time. Sales is a one-shot-only opportunity, blow it and it's gone. Ultimately, sales success depends on three things. First, understanding how the client buys; second, understanding how the client wants the service to be carried out; and third, understanding the client's culture. In achieving the third, the first two become easier to assess because the culture, together with its norms of behaviour, points to both a preferred intervention style and buying behaviour (Figure 6.2). Combining this with techniques such as SPIN® selling will improve the consultant's selling capability.

In the end, though, it is practice that makes perfect, and consultants need to experience the sales process in all of the four cultures to learn the subtleties of each. It should come as no real surprise that the majority of consultancies prefer to sell into the networked culture, as this is generally the most comfortable. Unfortunately, we also have to improve at selling into the others. The use of the after-action review technique described in Chapter 5 is of particular relevance during the sales process, irrespective of whether the sale was won or lost.

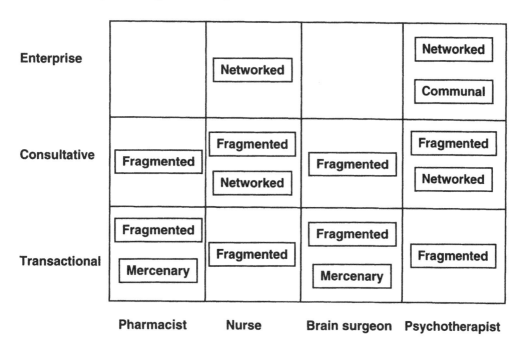

Figure 6.2   Preferred intervention styles and buying behaviours

7 Engagements and engagement management

A consultancy intervention should be an unique growth opportunity for all involved. When a consultant leaves the client premises for the last time, the client and the management team should be more capable of dealing with future uncertainties as well as today's emerging needs.[1]

Engagements begin when the consultants finally meet the client, and it is here where cultural intelligence is the most crucial. An engagement usually follows a standard pattern. It begins with the vanguard, those consultants who are initially sold into the client to deliver a small assignment. This is usually followed by a build up of consultancy staff, either working on the original project that was sold, or being brought in to carry out additional assignments that have been sold by the vanguard team. As discussed in Chapter 6, this farming activity is generally much easier than hunting for first-time clients, and if managed carefully can add value to the client and create a significant revenue stream for the consulting firm.

The nature of engagements and engagement management processes

Assignments usually become engagements when they involve more than just a handful of consultants. Although consultants are usually self-starters and require little if any direct supervision, as team size increases the need to formalize the processes across the team becomes essential. Finally the consulting team will peak in numbers and will eventually fade away, or a small number of consultants will remain working on small assignments for the client as a means of maintaining presence. In many instances, the remaining consultants often become the account managers of the future, as they know more about the client than anyone else in the firm.

The client's culture will influence the nature and length of engagements. As we saw in Chapter 5, organizations that have a communal culture are more likely to want a long-term consulting presence because they prefer a relationship based upon shared commitment and trust. Contrast this with organizations with a mercenary culture, which are more interested in limiting the engagement to the bare minimum. They are not interested in developing a long-term relationship; they want the job done and the consultants to leave. This type of understanding is essential during the account management and sales phases of the consulting life cycle, and will form the basis of designing the engagement.

There are three types of engagement:

- transactional

- those that are geared to opening new accounts
- those that are part of a mature, ongoing client relationship.

Within transactional engagements, the purpose is to complete the project and then leave without having any further client contact. Typical of this type of engagement would be an organizational or project review, the installation of an IT system, or the completion of a discrete piece of strategy work. In all cases, the engagement team is principally brought in for its technical skills, and does not expect to be with the client for more than a few months. Those engagements that are designed to penetrate a new account are usually short term and focused in order to establish client credibility. The purpose of the engagement is to establish a foothold within the client and from this win other work to build up the consultancy's presence. The firm would usually field a core team that would remain within the client for the duration of the engagement, which in some cases can extend into years. The core team would usually be augmented with additional fee earners with the appropriate industry, service and product expertise. During the lifetime of the engagement the physical number of consultants on site will vary considerably and reflect the level of activity across the client. The final form of engagement is one that falls within a mature, ongoing client relationship. In this instance it will arise from an expanding key account, or may occur when a dormant key account begins to stir.

Engagements involve a number of client-facing and firm-facing processes. Typical client-facing processes include:

- Client management: this is usually focused on the management of the contract, progress against the engagement plan and ensuring that any issues that arise as the engagement progresses are satisfactorily dealt with. This is especially important during the early stages of the engagement when the consultants and client are getting used to each other.
- Setting the scope of the engagement once on site and signing this off with the client: in many cases the sale is made on an overview of the problem and the proposed solution. What was said at the sale has to be translated into a fully fledged engagement, with plans, staff and action. Developing a common understanding of the full extent of the problem and of the detailed plans to resolve it is an essential first step in the engagement.
- Account management: the engagement manager will work with the account manager (who may or may not be working on the engagement) to assess and target other opportunities as the engagement progresses.
- Billing: this is a major process within the engagement and is often one of the most problematic, especially if the client is dissatisfied with the work of the consultancy. In general, the frequency of billing needs to be established either when the contract is finalized, or during the first few days of the engagement. Billing can be based on the satisfactory completion of engagement milestones, split regularly across the engagement's timeframe, or be based on the value derived from the engagement (often known as contingent fees). This latter approach is becoming more popular with firms as a way of reducing the initial costs of the consultancy to the client, but increasing the total fee income, based on the benefits of the engagement. For example, if a cost-reduction engagement is sold to a client, some of the fees may be contingent on the cost-savings identified by the consultancy actually materializing. And if the savings exceed those agreed, further fee income is possible.
- Maintaining engagement documentation: the importance of this cannot be overstated because of the need to manage risk. Because consultants are often brought in to address

difficult problems, there is always an element of risk associated with failing to deliver to client expectation. Processes such as account management and engagement management help to reduce the risk. But, in order to minimize risk still further all documentation associated with the engagement should be captured. Such documentation includes fee notes, letters of engagement, work package descriptions, relevant emails, key outputs such as meeting minutes, progress reports and so on. The engagement team should hold these centrally. And if the engagement is large it is best to use administrators rather than tie up fee-earning consultants. This documentation is not only used to manage the engagement but also to refer to if the client is concerned about progress. In general, the structure of engagement documentation would look like Figure 7.1. The engagement letter would open the umbrella under which the client and consultant would work. Then, depending on the size of the engagement, there could be a number of major work streams, each containing a number of discrete work packages. It is at the work-package level that the detailed information about what is to be done and by whom it is captured (Figure 7.2).

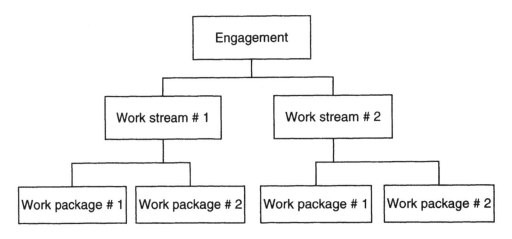

Figure 7.1   Engagement structure

With respect to the firm-facing engagement processes, these tend to be associated with the internal management of the account, staff assignments and appraisals, and chasing unpaid bills. The principal firm-facing processes are:

- Objective-setting and appraisals: every consultant is measured and rewarded against their performance. Therefore every assignment they undertake needs to be appraised by the engagement manager, or someone within the engagement team who is responsible for the consultant's work.
- Internal reporting: the engagement manager will usually report progress to the account manager or partner. These meetings are designed to discuss client and team issues. Within long-term engagements, rolling existing team-members off the account and bringing in new ones is an important process and one that requires careful management. In addition the engagement manager needs to gauge the morale of the team, as sustained periods of intense activity on an engagement can take their toll. Indeed, it is not uncommon for consultants to experience burnout on long intensive engagements.
- Client satisfaction and quality control: most consultancies depend on establishing solid

Work package name:	The name the assignment will be known as		Version: 1.0
Period covered: Start: End:		**Status:** Proposed or agreed	

Background:
Describes the background to the work package and why it has been decided to progress it

Objectives:
Lists the objectives that have been agreed between the client and consultant

Approach:
Describes how the work will be executed

Areas within scope: Identifies those areas of the assignment that the consultant/team will be responsible for	**Areas out of scope:** Identifies everything (in broad terms) that falls outside the assignment, and for which the consultant/team will not be responsible

Value added:
Indicates how the assignment will add value to the client (can be in terms of money, resolving a problem, bringing expertise to the client and so on)

Client deliverables/assumptions:

Description Describes all major deliverables (reports, software and so on)	Responsibility Highlights who in the client and the consultancy are responsible for completing the deliverables identified	Target date Date for completion

Client dependencies/assumptions:

Description Describes all assumptions made by the consultancy in relation to what is expected of the client; also details any dependencies on the client, such as availability of staff, senior management involvement and so on	Responsibility Identifies who within the client is responsible for ensuring its commitment within the work package is met	Target date Dates where necessary

Resource estimates:

Name	Total days	Start date	End date
Firm			
Client			

Approvals:	Name	Date	Signature
Client Sponsor			
Client fund holder			
Consultancy			

Figure 7.2   Work package template

working relationships with their clients. This in turn relies on the ability to deliver high-quality and valued services. Unsurprisingly firms go to a lot of trouble to capture client perspectives and opinions about the work they do for them. Client satisfaction surveys in which the client rates the consultants, their work and the value derived from the engagement are the primary methods of capturing such information. If results are below average the firm will investigate the reasons why, and feed this into their engagement management and consultant development processes. In extreme cases this can result in the issuing of credit notices that the client can use in future assignments. Within large engagements, consultancies typically conduct an internal quality assurance review, which involves senior members of the firm assessing engagement documentation, interviewing clients and meeting with members of the engagement team. The review will be used to assess quality, value, client satisfaction and engagement team morale. It will also identify any issues that require action from the account manager, engagement manager or the wider firm.

Building the engagement team

When building the engagement team, there is merit in considering the roles each team member will play and how these might fit the culture of the client. I believe that combining Belbin roles (see Table 7.1 for descriptions) with the four cultures can provide a useful insight as to who is needed on the team to get the best performance.

Table 7.1   Belbin roles

Belbin role	Description
Plant	Creative, imaginative, unorthodox. Solves difficult problems
Resource investigator	Extrovert, enthusiastic, communicative. Explores opportunities and develops contacts
Co-ordinator	Mature, confident. Clarifies goals. Brings other people together to promote team discussions
Shaper	Challenging, dynamic. Thrives on pressure. Has the drive and courage to overcome obstacles
Monitor/evaluator	Serious minded, strategic, discerning. Sees all options, and judges accurately
Team worker	Co-operative, mild, perceptive, diplomatic. Listens, builds, averts friction
Implementer	Disciplined, reliable, conservative in habits. Has a capacity for taking practical steps and actions
Completer/finisher	Painstaking, conscientious, anxious. Searches out errors and omissions. Delivers on time
Specialist	Single-minded, self-starting, dedicated. Provides knowledge and skills in rare supply.

When building the engagement team it is important to consider which Belbin role should be primary, secondary and tertiary:

- the primary role is performed by individuals who lead and build

- the secondary role is performed by individuals who get the job done
- tertiary roles are performed by those who add specialist one-off qualities and skills to a project.

Table 7.2 indicates which Belbin role suits which position in each of the four cultures. Pulling the team together successfully will depend on the level of analysis carried out by the engagement manager as the team is formed, and on whether the firm values such analysis.

Table 7.2   Belbin and the four cultures

Culture	Primary role	Secondary role	Tertiary role
Networked	Shaper	Resource investigator	Co-ordinator
Communal	Plant	Completer/finisher	Team worker
Mercenary	Completer/finisher	Implementer	Monitor/evaluator
Fragmented	Shaper	Monitor/evaluator	Specialist

Preparing the engagement team

One of the most important and yet neglected processes in any engagement is the preparation of the consultants prior to their joining the team. Consultants often have to muddle through wasting valuable time trying to sense how to work with the engagement team and the client. This creates unnecessary stress for both the consultant and the client. It is far better to screen consultants for their suitability prior to joining the engagement, and, if they are to join, provide them with enough information about the client, their culture and the engagement to make them feel comfortable about the work they will be undertaking and the people they will be working with (client and fellow consultants). This can be achieved by preparing briefing notes for all prospective consultants so that they can understand the key aspects of the client and engagement before joining. Such a briefing note should cover:

- client background, which should outline key facts and information about the client, its business, structure, performance and strategies
- client culture, which should identify which of the four cultures the client falls into
- key stakeholders, which should identify each major stakeholder in the client, provide a brief pen picture of them, including their role and position; in addition, it is often a good idea to state who from the engagement team is managing them from a relationship management perspective (see Chapter 8)
- engagement background, which should describe how the engagement came about, why it is important to the client, what it is intending to achieve and what involvement the consultancy has, both in terms of scope of work and numbers of consultants involved
- working patterns and expected behaviours, which should include how to work with the client (taking into account their culture), what is expected of the consultants, the structure of the engagement team, working hours, expense policies, time recording and so on.

It is this last element that is probably the most important to the consultant, as it provides the rules of engagement when working with the client and helps to reduce the likelihood of making errors of judgement. Table 7.3 summarizes the behaviours that should be adopted when working within each of the four cultures. As we saw in Chapter 2, when the engagement involves working with overseas clients, it is essential to extend this to cover the national dimension.

Table 7.3   Getting the behaviours right

Networked	Communal	Mercenary	Fragmented
• Make friends all over the organization • Help others when they need it • Be prepared to discuss and accept other people's interpretations of what you are doing and the rules of engagement • Make time to talk and be prepared for small talk – a certain degree of socializing is accepted • Don't talk down the company: people in general are very loyal • Be patient and tolerant with others • Accept ambiguity • Don't expect immediate decisions; consensus is important	• Join the family: make yourself part of the team in the widest sense • Be passionate in what you do • Display a sense of urgency in your work • Deliver, and focus on the results • Celebrate other people's success • Display sympathy and empathy for those that fail • Don't politic • Don't be cynical about the client • Be prepared to put the client above all else • Practise what you preach • Work hard and play hard – accept invitations to attend social events	• Make things happen • Keep your head down; you're here to work • Complete tasks once started • Hit your targets; poor performance is not tolerated • Don't spend too much time thinking, action is more important • Expect and embrace politics • Don't bullshit • Focus on the short term • Be prepared to be challenged on your work and to challenge others • Position is important • Expect poor levels of communication	• Make yourself valuable • Focus on ideas and outcomes, not individuals • Be prepared to work alone • Analytical behaviour is favoured over intuitive • Be self-critical of your work, and critical of the work of others • Don't expect to make friends • Tolerate idiosyncratic behaviour • Expect to work with the best, so don't assume you know everything

As the engagement progresses, the engagement manager should look out for signs of cultural misalignment within the engagement team. There will be occasions when consultants find it difficult to make the adjustments necessary to fit in with the client. Rather than allow this to continue the engagement manager must spend some time with the person concerned to understand any issues they might have. And if the consultant feels unable to make the necessary adjustments, he or she should be rolled off the engagement. It is generally better to remove people from the account early, than allow them to cause further damage to the client–consultant relationship. This type of action should be rare where the engagement team has been culturally prepared beforehand.

Managing engagements within the four cultures

Engagements can be considered to be a collection of small and medium-sized projects, and, in the case of large engagements, programmes. Although the nature of the engagement will vary considerably, there are some underlying cultural aspects that require an appropriate response from the engagement manager and their consulting teams. For example, in some circumstances the visibility of the project management processes will have to be hidden from view because they would be seen to be an unnecessary overhead. Of course, processes still have to be applied, but in some cases these have to remain invisible to the client. The skill of the engagement and project manager is to ensure they use processes and techniques wisely and brief their team carefully. Engagements and their associated projects will require a particular emphasis in order for them to be successful (Figure 7.3).

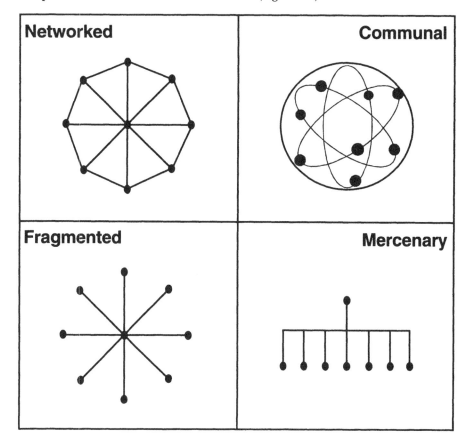

Figure 7.3   Managing projects in the four cultures

NETWORKED

Within the networked culture, the emphasis should be on managing the wider stakeholder community. The engagement should carefully map out the stakeholders and determine how best to use them to achieve the engagement's goals. This will involve exploiting the natural means of getting things done in this type of organization. Engagements within networked organizations should be communication-rich, with focus placed on the changes that will occur at the individual level, especially in relation to roles and responsibilities. This is because people matter in the networked culture. And for the engagement to be successful, everyone needs to feel involved. It is essential that the engagement team takes trouble to meet as many of the client staff as possible so that they become perceived to be part of the client team, rather than external consultants to be viewed suspiciously. This helps to eliminate the perception that the consultants are imposing their solution onto the staff.

It is likely that the networked organization will have project-management processes in place, and these will usually be followed religiously. Methods and tools should therefore be visible and carefully applied, as this organization does not like to take short cuts. Following due process is therefore important, and the networked organization will expect the consultancy to either adopt its processes or bring in its own. Of course, the use of methods and tools does not guarantee success. Indeed it is usual to find methods and tools being applied inconsistently with very few people using them in the way they were intended.

Because the networked culture values consensus it is important to agree what has to be done and when, particularly when there are major decisions to be made. As a result the engagement may take longer than was originally anticipated. This highlights one of the key dangers within the networked culture: the length of time it takes to get things done, as meetings, debates and briefings will create a significant cost driver. Therefore the engagement manager and their team must have the diplomatic skills to move the project on at an appropriate pace whilst still allowing sufficient debate. In some cases this will mean relying on the client's movers and shakers to unblock barriers and get things moving (identified during the stakeholder analysis). This is where the networked culture comes into its own, because there will be plenty of people who will be willing to help. However, despite such enthusiasm, commitment is not always matched with action. This lack of action highlights a distinct problem within the networked culture around the knowing–doing gap. This is where a problem is acknowledged but no one is willing to tackle it – there tends to be plenty of discussion about what needs to be done, but without concerted action and ownership, organizing committees, working parties and brainstorming sessions will not resolve the problem in hand. The fallback for the networked culture is inaction. This tends to spill over into the general working environment, where people busy themselves without really delivering very much. And because the majority of staff within the networked culture lack stretching work there is a degree of dumbing down that exacerbates this problem. It is here that the consultant can add significant value by taking control and providing leadership where there is no drive to complete.

COMMUNAL

Within the communal culture, the emphasis will be on managing the boundary. Because the communal culture is focused on achievement, taking risks and passion, the significant danger for the engagement is non-completion, over-engineering and getting sidetracked with interesting diversions instead of sticking to the core deliverables required to complete the project successfully. Indeed, everyone will be keen to explore new avenues, but to ensure this does not waste too much time, the engagement manager will need to keep on their toes to achieve closure. Failure to do so could jeopardize the whole engagement, as it will fail to deliver within the schedule set out at the start, and may end up delivering something totally different. This genre of problem was very clear in the dotcom business start-ups. These start-ups were so focused on being first to market with their website and developing their overly optimistic sales projections that they failed to address some of the fundamental business issues they faced. Considerations such as who was going to buy their products, how much advertising would cost, could their technology cope with expected demand and so on were ill thought out and badly planned. They got carried away with the concept and their vision without bringing it back down to earth and taking a long hard look at its viability. This reflects the way the communal culture perceives risk. It does not exist in its vocabulary. As a result it does not like anyone who is risk-averse, as this is perceived to be an excuse for inaction. Of course, risk management is a key element to all engagements, and the skill is to manage the risks without appearing to be risk-averse.

Communal organizations usually lack even the basic project management disciplines, and will not care for detailed process. Therefore, it is essential for the consultant to use basic project management disciplines to ensure the engagement remains on track and is not overtaken by events. That said, the communal organization recognizes that discipline is necessary to get the job done and will accept the need for project management expertise. Engagements within a communal culture will be fast and focused, and involve lots of creativity and ideas. Once set in motion they can be very hard to stop, as people will get carried away. In order to address these risks it is advisable to use time-boxing and rapid development techniques throughout the project. Fast-paced change is the norm, and that is why process is of little concern.

Everyone in the engagement team must show strong commitment to the client organization, and not just in terms of delivering the engagement. It is important for the engagement team to socialize with the client after the working day has finished. This helps to develop strong ties and ensures the client feels the consultancy is committed to its organization. For example I was working with a client overseas that had a strong communal culture. Everyone in the client company passionately believed in what they were trying to achieve, and it was important for me and the engagement team to do likewise. To demonstrate this shared belief it was necessary to take a detailed interest in the organization, its mission and its people. It also meant creating the boundary around the programme of work so that the inherent risks could be managed (albeit invisibly at times). In addition, it meant becoming part of the family and joining in the social events of the client. One of our team was culturally insensitive and managed to upset the client by being overly risk-averse and taking no time to understand its business or culture. This person viewed the client as a transaction rather than a long-term relationship, which was clearly inappropriate for a communal culture. There was also a perception that this person was devious and untrustworthy. Resolving the issue took a considerable amount of time and effort, which would have been unnecessary had the person acted in a culturally sensitive way at the start of the engagement.

MERCENARY

As with the communal culture, the mercenary culture also shuns process and project management disciplines. For example, it may talk about how important project management is, but the culture does not permit it to be used much, if at all. This is because the mercenary culture is focused on action, not planning. It is a 'ready, aim, fire' culture. Furthermore, those required to provide input into the engagement will often resist involvement, especially if this takes them away from their day-to-day work. This is because people are rewarded for action, through bonuses, promotions and so on. They are not rewarded for talking about what they will do; rhetoric counts for nothing in the mercenary culture. Therefore they will only become engaged in the project if there is a direct link between the engagement outcome and their personal reward (both in a positive and negative sense). Avoiding the problems that this lack of commitment presents means adopting a command and control approach to the management of the engagement. Strong reporting lines and links into a powerful sponsor will be necessary, as this person will be needed to apply sanctions when progress is slow.

Projects within mercenary cultures are fast paced and ill planned, and can often wither on the vine. This latter point is important, because in mercenary organizations the project team is often the last to know that there is no longer any interest in their project. Mercenary organizations can be likened to bees around a honey pot: lots of interest in the short term, but if something more exciting comes along, such as the next crisis, people lose interest and move on to the next thing. This has important implications for the engagement team as it goes about its work. Maintaining the commitment of the client staff can be difficult at times and there are likely to be significant political barriers to overcome. Unfortunately, the senior management within the client will expect the consultants to resolve these types of problems without much intervention from themselves. And if things don't go according to plan it will be the consultants who will be blamed. So managing politics within the mercenary culture is a key activity for the engagement team.

As with the communal culture, methods, tools and processes are disliked. So expecting people to comply with planning standards and so on is pointless. The skill of the project manager in the mercenary culture is therefore to make things happen using whatever methods they can, and by keeping them invisible. If this means using spreadsheets, lists or Microsoft Project, then so be it. Mercenary organizations only value delivery, not the process you need to go through. Therefore, don't expect the mercenary culture to have any project management standards, processes or tools. Even if they do possess such things no one will be using them because they will be perceived as an unnecessary barrier to getting things done. Ironically, of course, having nothing in place usually means projects take longer, are more prone to failure and are very inefficient.

FRAGMENTED

Fragmented cultures are probably the most difficult to run projects within because of the fiefdoms that exist. Unlike the other three cultures, the fragmented culture does not have any unifying corporate mission that people buy into. And even in those cases where there is such a thing, the fiefdoms rarely comply. This means everything tends to be run locally, and according to local and personal need. Therefore, whenever an engagement spans the whole organization, the engagement manager must be able to create the perception that the engagement is making each individual function shine. This is the classic win–win approach, and it is essential that the consultant meets each major stakeholder to establish what he or she wants out of the engagement, and develop the relationship management and delivery strategies accordingly. One such strategy could be to establish mini-projects for each area of the business and tie these into a single plan. In this way the individual needs of the stakeholders can be met, whilst still achieving the overall organizational objectives. This may, of course, require a larger project team than usual, but it is a useful way to achieve a successful outcome.

Although the fragmented culture is poor on communication, it is vital that the consultancy team maintains high levels of contact throughout the engagement in order to transfer ideas and intelligence, and discuss progress and client issues. This will ensure that the account manager is able to keep a clear view of what is happening in the account and of the opportunities that are presenting themselves. It will also allow the team to avoid some of the many political pitfalls that will exist between their respective projects and client contacts.

The use of methods and tools is essential in fragmented organizations, and they have to be visible to maintain a clear direction and sense of progress. In particular, the use of risk and issue processes is one way to tie everyone in, as no one within the organization wants to be seen to be failing. If we recall what fragmented cultures expect of their consultants, we can understand why the use of methods, tools and experts is essential. After all, the team should be making the client shine and to do so, in their eyes at least, this will mean applying methods and process visibly. It will also mean fielding a senior team that has the experience, grey hair and scars to demonstrate its ability. More than any other, the fragmented culture dislikes the junior consultant with no in-depth knowledge or experience.

Dealing with politics

Politics should be expected in any engagement, and dealing with its various dimensions is a core skill of the consultant. Whereas many of the client's staff complain of the political nature of their workplace and shy away from it, it is essential that the consultant takes the trouble to understand the politics of the client and be prepared to embrace and apply it during the delivery of the engagement. There are three underlying reasons why politics exists within organizations:[2]

- Competition for scarce or prized resources: this includes physical resources, such as equipment and office space, as well as human capital, position and status. It is not uncommon to see political problems arise within projects that require the same skilled resource as the operational line, nor is it surprising to see arguments and back-stabbing associated with roles, responsibilities and positions within organizations. In both circumstances, there would be no politics if resources were in abundant supply or there was no real competition for positions of power.
- Self-interest: although there are many people within organizations who place organizational interests above their own, there is a significant minority that will pursue a path of self-interest. This may mean appearing to do the right thing for the organization, but it is usually masking ulterior motives. Such self-interest should not be overlooked within an engagement, and, if anything, it should be surfaced as quickly as possible and actively addressed.
- Power and the struggle to achieve it. The feeling of having no power is unbearable to the majority of people, and where an engagement is altering the balance of power a political reaction should be expected. Interestingly, nothing has really changed since the times of the mediaeval court. Here the courtiers had to be elegant, committed and friendly, whilst scheming and plotting in the background. Overt power plays were frowned upon and could end up in imprisonment or death. Today the same rules apply: people must appear civilized, decent, democratic and fair, but none of us can take these rules too literally, as we will be crushed by those who are plotting around us. Therefore it is naïve to expect full commitment and buy-in from the client during the engagement. Just because large sums of money are being spent on the consultancy does not mean that everyone believes in

what it is attempting to achieve. Robert Greene has written an excellent book, *The 48 laws of power*,[3] which should be a mandatory read for all consultants. Within it he highlights the types of actions that are commonly adopted by individuals who pursue power. This not only helps consultants to prepare themselves for the types of power-related issues they face, but it also allows them to use some of the techniques themselves during the engagement. I will highlight the power laws applicable to each culture in the next chapter.

In order to manage politics it is first necessary to identify and analyse it. This can be achieved using the following four steps:[4]

1. Identify the activities and actions that are associated with the organization's scarce and prized resources. Political infighting typically occurs around such things as change projects, technology investments, research and development, and product development, Increasingly, the reduction in the number of senior management positions within organizations has led to much higher stakes for those who seek the trappings of power. As a result there is significantly more political infighting between those who wish to become the senior managers of the future. Once the sources of political battles have been identified it is necessary to identify everyone who is involved, as this will help to frame the extent of the political landscape that has to be managed within the engagement.
2. Identify the motivations behind competitive activities. Successfully managing politics requires the identification of the motivations of those involved. Therefore the creation of a stakeholder map that identifies the key relationships, rivalries and alliances of those touched by the engagement is a key activity during the first few weeks (see Chapter 8).
3. Identify the sources of power. Power resides in five fundamental forms. Positional power is the legitimized power that exists in a person's position within an organization. Status power exists by virtue of the title people are given, even when they have no real positional power; for example, non-executive directors would fall into this category. Resource power resides in anyone who manages or owns scarce resource. Such people have probably the strongest source of power – that associated with veto. Although they may be quite low within the organization's hierarchy, they can wield significant power over the success of an engagement. The final source of power is that associated with expertise: the guru or subject-matter expert can be a powerful figure in any organization.
4. Assess the political strategies adopted by those who seek power or scarce resources. For completeness, I have included some of the common political strategies used within organizations (Table 7.4).[5] It should be remembered, of course, that these political behaviours are essentially about power, either its acquisition or retention. They are especially important within the context of a consultancy engagement because of the damage they can cause. Valuable time can be wasted on trying to gain buy-in from reluctant functional units, seeking out vital information on which the engagement depends, or gaining access to senior managers. All of these sap the engagement's energy, and, of course, are usually deliberate moves to limit its impacts. However, the engagement team must recognize that it too can use some of these strategies to tackle political opponents.

As expected, politics within each of the four cultures will vary considerably, and it is important for the engagement team to understand the specific nature of politics in each. This will have implications for the composition of the engagement team as well as how relationships are managed within the client.

Table 7.4   Political behaviours

Political behaviour	Description
Ownership	An individual or group owns a project, product line, department, process, and benefits from the status and rights of ownership. Ownership is all about control by being there first. Within projects, it is the ownership of resources that typically creates the greatest amount of political turbulence.
Information manipulation	Knowledge is power. More information generates more filters through which the information must pass, and each filter provides ample opportunity for information distortion. Typical tactics include withholding information, and manipulating it to change the message (for example distorting bad news to appear good, or not divulging it). Information manipulation is increasingly linked to ownership.
Alliances	Political battles within organizations usually involve taking sides, and a consultancy engagement is no different. Types of behaviour include those associated with sycophants, sleepers (waiting to join the winning side), shoulder rubbers (face-to-face contacts), and those that monopolize others' time.
Invisible walls	These are especially applicable to engagements where rules, procedures and information access are placed in the path of the engagement to slow it down, derail it and generally prevent it from achieving its objectives. The invisible-wall game is best played by those who can maintain the appearance of sincere effort, but without actually achieving anything.
Strategic non-compliance	Agreeing up front to co-operate, and defaulting on the agreement at the last minute, leaving little or no opportunity for the other party to do anything about it.
Discrediting	It is said that reputation is one of the cornerstones of power, and once lost is almost impossible to regain. Therefore, discrediting individuals is one of the surest ways to gain power.
Camouflage	The purpose of camouflage is to distract or confuse people long enough to defuse or deflect a course of action. This type of behaviour within engagements would usually result in the engagement team hunting down needless information, at the project's expense. Camouflage can sometimes be associated with discrediting.

NETWORKED

Although the networked organization exudes friendliness, don't be fooled into believing that there will be no politics. But because of the nature of the networked culture, political battles will be fought in a gentlemanly fashion with each party being careful not to display any outward signs of their political agendas. Yet behind the scenes there will be plenty of scheming and back-stabbing going on. And those that choose to use politics tend to be very smart at its application. They have to be because the organization does not like politics and tends to shy away from it. As a result they learn to apply their craft so well that many do not realize that they have been discredited or outmanoeuvred. Their success ultimately relies on their creation and use of a personal network of supporters and spies across the organization. Some may be personal friends; others may be sycophants and hangers-on. Modern office technology such as email allows plots to be hatched with ease, particularly through the blind copying of emails. In order to sensitize the engagement team to the politics that exists within the networked organization, the creation of a stakeholder map that identifies, amongst other things, the key players and their allies, their enemies and how they perceive the engagement is very useful. The results of this analysis will allow the engagement team to develop their strategies for dealing with those that wish to see the engagement fail. The other aspect to politics within the networked culture that often requires intervention is where the sponsor is politically naïve. Because such people shy away from the political turf wars that inevitably accompany change, the role of politician often falls to the consultant.

COMMUNAL

In general politics is frowned upon within the communal culture because everyone believes in the firm's mission and is more than willing to work together to achieve it. As a result, the engagement team must avoid taking political decisions or making negative comments about personalities or the organization as a whole. A rather dim view will be taken of this, and it will affect the credibility of the team and potentially the engagement. This is probably the most refreshing culture to work within because of the absence of politics.

MERCENARY

Within mercenary organizations politics equates to open warfare, as no one hides their feelings about their colleagues. Because it's a dog-eat-dog culture that is focused on achievement, everyone recognizes that you are only as good as your last project and there is always someone else to take over when you leave. As a consequence everyone is looking over their shoulders. In this environment the engagement team should expect a rough ride and be prepared for frank exchanges within meetings as well as within the team. Surviving the politics within mercenary organizations involves spotting where the power lies and using relationships to gain support and remove the opposition. It's first-strike kill, so you have to be willing to take out the competition before they take you and your team out. In mercenary organizations the greatest danger, however, lies with aligning the engagement with a single powerful sponsor, who may not be around forever.

The only advantage of politics within the mercenary organization is that it is laid bare before you, and as long as the team has the stomach to deal with it, politics can be straightforward. It is useful to bear in mind that within the mercenary culture there will be plenty of hot air and little substance to most of the political statements made. Someone's bark is usually worse than their bite, and most back down when they are challenged. Ironically, this pushback (or challenge) is precisely what the clients want to see from their consultants. Perceiving such people as playground bullies is not a bad coping strategy. Stand up to them and they crumble. Successfully dealing with the political angle requires a dual strategy of delivering against the engagement plan and playing the politics between the major players. It is also essential to hedge your bets to ensure that the engagement team is not caught in the crossfire. For example, whilst working on an assignment in an investment bank I had to endure a number of weeks of political infighting. I was able to survive by continuing to deliver, creating my own network of allies and playing one senior manager off against another. Unfortunately, a colleague of mine who found himself in a similar position was not quite so successful. He was asked to leave the engagement. He viewed politics as something to be avoided, rather than something that had to be actively managed. More than any of the other three cultures, it is the mercenary one where you ignore politics at your peril.

FRAGMENTED

Politics within fragmented organizations tends to fester under the surface, and open displays such as those found within mercenary organizations are very rare. Instead most of the political deals are struck behind closed doors. This makes it is impossible to see political problems coming unless care is taken to establish friends across the organization who are willing to share intelligence. The members of the engagement team must therefore take time to sensitize themselves to the politics of the client by establishing a number of contacts across the organization. In some instances, it will be necessary to play one stakeholder off against another to ensure success. If this is done carefully, neither will recognize your role in the political manoeuvring. This is much easier to achieve in the fragmented culture than either the networked or mercenary cultures because no network exists through which the client can gather its own intelligence. The special position of the consultant, who has to seek views across the organization, can be the best way to deal with politics. Recalling that fragmented organizations are a collection of individual fiefdoms, it should come as little surprise that most hate each other and relish the opportunity for politicking.

THE CULTURALLY INTELLIGENT ENGAGEMENT MANAGER

- understands the basic cultural differences of the four client cultures and what this means for the structure of the engagement
- ensures the engagement team is fully prepared before going on site; this will be achieved by preparing an engagement team brief that describes how each member of the team should behave within the client
- will take immediate action to address misaligned behaviour within the engagement team, if necessary removing team members from the engagement
- will take time to understand the key behaviours within their client, including those associated with politics and power, and develop strategies for managing the political issues they are likely to face within the engagement
- tailors the consultancy's products and services to suit the client culture.

When engagements lose control[6]

As we saw with the Westpac CS90 project, engagements can go horribly wrong, and although it is difficult to find out information about them, there is plenty of anecdotal evidence to suggest that significant problems can occur. One of the few books that dares to highlight such failures is *Dangerous company*, which discusses some of the most significant, including:

- Figgie International, which between 1989 and 1994 spent more than $75 million on consulting fees with the major players (Andersen Consulting, Boston Consulting Group, Deloitte and Touche, and a host of others) only to find its business ruined[7]
- O'Neal Steel Company, which ended up taking Andersen Consulting to court over the failure of a technology project that was designed to bring its operating structure and customer service department up to the 21st century[8]
- an IBM Consulting engagement at Hershey Foods in the United States, which resulted in its supply chain being tied up in knots; the company lost shelf space at retailers, and its share price dropped 22 per cent over the course of 1999.[9]

Although consulting engagements fail because of a lack of cultural intelligence, there is one major factor that is associated with any large and costly undertakings (including consultancy engagements) which has to be managed. This is to do with over-commitment or escalation:

> Escalation refers to a predicament where decision makers find themselves trapped in a losing course of action as a result of previous decisions. Costs are incurred; there is an opportunity to withdraw or to persist; and the consequences of withdrawal or persistence are uncertain. Typically, the response of such dilemmas is irrational persistence.[10]

It is well known that to deliver any major engagement successfully depends on a sustained level of commitment from the consultants and client. Commitment provides the necessary level of energy and enthusiasm to make the engagement a success. However, no matter how vital, organizations and consultancies can sometimes become overcommitted to an engagement, to the point where they ignore some of the basic warning signs that it is failing. Such excessive commitment, termed escalation, also prevents the decision to terminate the engagement from being made early enough. In such circumstances, organizations continue to sink additional money and resources into the engagement, and in doing so increases their commitment to it. This creates a vicious circle of increasing commitment, costs and probability of failure.

Therefore, as well as the engagement risks associated with organizational complexity, firms also have to deal with issues associated with individual responsibility, and accountability and escalation. And it is essential that they recognize the warning signs and take corrective action before the engagement begins to lose control. This is not easy because the nature of risk has become more complex, and the consequences more significant. As a result people (clients and consultants) have become less willing to raise risks early enough to allow them to be effectively managed, mainly because they are worried about the personal consequences. This can be a major problem for consultancies that never expect their staff to fail. Moreover, with an 'up or out' culture the majority of consultants will hide the truth in the hope that they can cover up or resolve the problem without the client finding out.

Irrational behaviour that lies at the heart of escalation can be viewed at three distinct levels – the individual, the group and the senior executive. This extra level has been included because the positional power of the senior executive allows the intensity of the irrational behaviours to be amplified. Although it can be argued that the behaviours identified at this level are equally applicable to the individual level, it is power that makes them more damaging.

INDIVIDUAL BEHAVIOUR

- *Availability error*: the most recent material is 'available'. Previous knowledge and data are lost in the immediacy of the event. Not surprisingly, this type of irrational behaviour is often stimulated by dramatic events.
- *Halo effect*: the tendency to see all personal attributes consistently. For example, a good sportsman is expected to be a good businessman or father, indeed good at everything. The reverse can also apply, where someone is classed as being a general all-round poor performer.
- *Primacy error*: beliefs formed by first impressions, with later evidence interpreted in light of this initial impression. The adage 'first impression counts' is applicable here. If powerful, primacy error can generate positive or negative halo effects very early on within a relationship.
- *Conformity error*: conformance of an individual to the behaviour of others whether they know they are making a mistake by doing so, or whether they are unaware both of their mistake and of the social pressure that has induced them to make it.

GROUP BEHAVIOUR

- *Groups*: where group members' attitudes are biased in one direction, the interaction of the group will tend to increase this bias because of the need to be valued and suppress criticism. Engaging in a common task only decreases hostility between groups if the outcome is successful. Where it is not, blame is passed from one group to the other, with any existing divisions widening.
- *Stereotypes*: these are convenient tools for assessing an individual who belongs to a group. As a result, rather than being expected to act individually, a member of a group is expected to conform to the stereotypical behaviour of the entire group. Therefore, no attempt is made at assessing an individual's behaviour in isolation from the rest of the group. Stereotypes tend to be self-fulfilling because of both primacy and availability errors.

SENIOR EXECUTIVE BEHAVIOUR

- *Public decisions*: these are more likely to be executed than those taken privately. In general people do not want to lose face, especially in public.
- *Misplaced consistency*: someone who has embarked on a course of action may feel they must continue to justify their initial decision. People who have made a sacrifice – time, effort or money – in order to do something tend to go on doing it, even when they stand to lose more than they could gain by continuing. There is always the hope that the situation can be retrieved, but this is rarely the case in practice.
- *Ignoring the evidence*: people tend to seek confirmation of their current hypothesis instead of trying to disconfirm it. In general, there is a refusal to look for contradictory evidence, or indeed believe or act upon it if it is brought to their attention.
- *Distorting the evidence*: evidence favouring a belief will strengthen it, whilst contradictory evidence is ignored. As a result the belief remains intact. Therefore, evidence that is contrary to a particular viewpoint will be distorted and dismissed as being irrelevant or inapplicable. Where the evidence is partially correct, it will be distorted to emphasize the positive aspects over the negative.

Engagement managers will need to be aware of these behaviours within themselves, their teams and their clients, and then act accordingly to address any overcommitment. Because consultants have such a can-do attitude and a supreme self-belief, overcommitment can be a real problem. Many will not see themselves overcommitting, and will work harder and longer rather than admit defeat. This is in part due to the performance criteria laid out in most consultants' annual appraisal. Failure is not accepted within consultancies, and those who do fail are likely either not to last long or at the very least to limit their career within the firm. A consultant's reputation is won or lost on every assignment. It's a macho culture where only the toughest survive. This would appear to be at odds with the networked-come-fragmented culture of the typical consultancy. But this is the dark side, the almost mercenary heart of the consulting model.

Fortunately there are a number of common attributes that suggest certain engagements are more likely to suffer from escalation than others. These are useful, as they can provide the engagement manager with an additional level of sensitivity to the problems of escalation. These attributes are:

- The imposition of tight and unrealistic timescales. This includes those imposed by the organization, and the consultancy in order to win the contract, or those that are the result of external market pressure – such as a sudden change in the economic climate, or the need to address regulatory requirements.
- The need for significant capital and non-capital investment.
- The expectation of significant returns on investment. This might be imposed by the organization through investment-appraisal hurdle rates, expected because of one or two high-profile, and well-publicized successes, or stated as achievable by a consultancy wanting to win the business.
- The use of leading-edge technologies (or technologies that are at the boundary of an organization's capability) to break into new markets, or to introduce major organizational change.
- The dependence of the future of the business on the successful outcome of the project, or where the project is considered business-critical. Such projects typically have to succeed, no matter what the cost.
- The dependence of senior managers' careers on the successful outcome of the project.
- The public announcement of the project, either within the organization, to the wider business population or, in the case of government projects, to the general population.

By way of illustration, I have included the following example of a failed software project that shows clearly how irrational behaviours of individuals, groups and senior executives can lead to the escalation of a project to the point of failure. To aid interpretation, the relevant irrational behaviours are given in bold type. With so many consulting projects having a strong technological component, readers would be well advised to take this example to heart.

In 1988 a consortium comprising Hilton National Hotels, Marriott and Budget Rent-A-Car initiated a large-scale project to develop a state-of-the-art travel-reservation system combining airline, car-rental and hotel information. The project was to be run by AMR Information Services (AMRIS), a subsidiary of American Airlines, whose previous experience of developing the SABRE airline reservation system had been highly successful (**halo effect**, **primacy error** and **availability error**). The project was originally split into two distinct phases – design and development – with the option to withdraw from the project (with a $1 million penalty) when the development plan was presented. The design phase was to last 7 months, and the development phase a further 37 months. The project was due to complete in June 1992, and the cost was not expected to exceed $55 million. In March 1989 the development plan, which followed the completion of the design in December 1988, was presented by AMRIS. This was considered to be unacceptable by the consortium, and was subsequently reworked by AMRIS over a period of 6 months. During this time AMRIS senior executives were at pains to reassure the consortium that all was well with the project. Although by this stage the project's costs had risen from $55 million to $72.6 million, and implementation had slipped to July 1992, the consortium agreed to continue, basing their decision on the expected returns (**misplaced consistency**). The project benefits went without challenge and were later found to be significantly at variance with those presented by AMRIS (**halo effect, primacy error**). Almost without exception, deadlines were missed and phases rescheduled, yet the software developers remained convinced they would be able to claw back the lost time and implement as planned (**ignoring the evidence**). Despite continued assurances from AMRIS that the project would meet its time and budgetary targets, it consistently missed major milestones in January and February 1990. At this time AMRIS admitted to being 13 weeks behind schedule, but still remained confident of meeting the deadlines. During the summer of 1990, two members of the consortium expressed severe concerns that the project would not be able to deliver within the remaining schedule. Although this was ratified by the project, they were instructed by management to change the dates to reflect the original plan, which they duly did (**distorting the evidence, misplaced consistency**, and **conformity error**). To that end AMRIS declared one part of the development phase complete in August 1990, but refused to show any of the deliverables to the consortium. In October 1990 the developers admitted to being over one year behind schedule, but insisted that they would be able to meet the original deadline (**misplaced consistency, ignoring the evidence**). In February 1991 AMRIS replanned the project, which resulted in further slippage and a phased implementation of system functionality. So although Hilton would receive all the functionality relevant to their requirements by June 1992, Marriott would not receive theirs until March 1993. Later, after the project was replanned, Marriott claimed that AMRIS forced employees to artificially change their timetable to reflect this new project plan, and those that refused were either reassigned to a new project or sacked (**distorting the evidence, groups**, and **conformity error**). By this time the price for the system had reached $92 million, significantly above the maximum of $55 million. In October 1991 the AMRIS president, along with a number of other AMRIS employees, resigned. A report by an external consultant was buried by the vice-president of AMRIS and the consultant dismissed because of dissatisfaction with the findings (**ignoring the evidence**). Despite all that had happened, and all evidence pointing to the non-delivery of the system, Marriott and Hilton were still willing to give AMRIS one last chance (**misplaced consistency**). AMRIS assured both that it was still able to meet the project's deadline (**ignoring the evidence**). Finally, in April 1992, AMRIS admitted it was between two and six months behind schedule, but it was not until major problems materialized during testing that they admitted the system would not be fully complete for at least another 18 months. This announcement was shortly followed by AMRIS sacking a number of top executives and employees. It was also acknowledged that members of the project team had not raised their concerns early enough, instead preferring to allow them to remain hidden (**conformity error, groups**).

When considering each of the four cultures and their susceptibility to escalation it is likely that they could all suffer. Communal organizations would be vulnerable because of their singular focus and strong desire to make things happen. They would never see the risks of escalation because they rarely see the downside of their actions, as we witnessed with the dotcoms. Mercenary organizations would fail to spot the warning signs because most people are worried about their tenure, and will hide any risks and issues rather then admit to them. Therefore, when anything starts to go wrong, their natural tendency is in fact to escalate, as we saw when Nick Leeson ran up huge debts at Barings, resulting in its subsequent failure. Fragmented organizations are unlikely to prevent escalation because no one sees it as 'their' problem, as we so often see in large government-sponsored projects and programmes. People will spend more time protecting their patch than preventing failure. And the networked organization is perhaps too friendly to raise such overcommitment as a problem. Instead employees are more willing to circle around the issue as it gets bigger and bigger until it is too large to deal with. Addressing escalation within a consulting engagement ultimately rests with the engagement manager. This is where having a degree of independence from the client helps. But it is also necessary to address the internal (consultancy) tendency to cover up failures.

When tackling escalation and the issues of failure, it is best to start the conversation with the consulting partners/senior executives to assess the implications for the engagement, the client relationship and obviously fee income. This is very important because it allows the consultancy to decide on the strategy that it will adopt when it meets the client to discuss the issue. Naturally there will be a number of options open, including reducing fees, providing the client with a credit note, withdrawing altogether and perhaps refocusing the engagement. Each of these will have implications and it is vital that they are fully explored prior to speaking to the client. The client, of course, might be aware that there are issues and will want to speak to the consultants as soon as possible to discuss the options. This discussion should involve the partners/senior executives of the firm plus the engagement manager (who should have all the facts to hand). The outcome of the meeting should of course be as amicable as possible.

Summary

Engagements are where the consultants meet the clients and spend weeks, months and maybe years working with them. Successful engagements can lead to significant onward sales for the consultancy and can add real value to the client. However, like any major intervention, they do not always run smoothly. This is often because the engagement manager and their team do not take care to tailor their behaviours, methods and tools to the client's culture. Understanding how to adjust behaviour is an essential but neglected component of engagement management, and consultancies would be wise to update their approach to incorporate cultural preparation. Consultancy can often involve the client investing significant sums in major change and technology projects. Like any large undertaking, there is a real danger that the client and consultant will overcommit to the engagement when it starts to go wrong. Knowing the warning signs and how to respond is another area that falls within the engagement manager's purview. In the last chapter of Part II, I will examine the final component of the consultancy process: relationship management.

8 *Relationship management*

[T]rust does not happen without work, without volition, or without effort. It is not handed to use on a platter . . . it must be borne in mind that trust results from accumulated experiences, over time. There is no quick fix.[1]

[T]rust is an expectation about the positive actions of other people, without being able to influence or monitor the outcome.[2]

Trust is the expectation that arises within a community of regular, honest and cooperative behavior, based on commonly shared norms, on the part of other members of that community.[3]

A few years ago, I was working on an engagement within a global investment bank. During a meeting with one of the managing directors, I saw a notice on the wall behind her (Figure 8.1).[4] It struck me that if you were to replace the word leader with consultant, it

---

Foundations of Trust

Trust, at its simplest level, can be defined as confidence in those on whom we depend. To build trust, organizations and their leaders must balance three key imperatives: achieving results, acting with integrity, and demonstrating concern.

Achieving Results. First and foremost, people trust those who are willing (because of their drive, discipline and commitment) and able (because of their knowledge, skills and courage) to deliver the results they promise. By contrast, we distrust those we consider misguided or incompetent. Anyone who cannot achieve the performance expectations that our organization imposes will be hard-pressed to earn trust.

Acting with Integrity. Integrity requires honesty in one's words and consistency in one's actions. People trust those who are direct in expressing their views and predictable in acting within a known set of principles. Inconsistency suggests that leaders are dishonest or self-serving. Those who conceal or distort the truth, or who constantly change their strategies and practices, are rarely trusted. The impact of integrity is paramount early in a relationship, as each side assesses the degree to which it can trust the other.

Demonstrating Concern. Fundamentally, trust requires that leaders understand and respect the interests of people at all levels and in all constituencies. More specifically, people trust those who consider their interests even in the face of potentially conflicting pressures. This does not require leaders to place our needs above all others. We do expect, however, that they will not deliberately take advantage of our reliance on them.

Figure 8.1 Trust

would sum up what relationship management within consultancy was all about. I felt at the time that if I couldn't display all of these attributes, it would be very difficult for me to deliver value to my current client. And looking at each of the three foundations it would suggest that all have a cultural element to them. Thus, although achieving results should be a given for all consultants, the way they are achieved will vary according to the underlying culture of the client. It is also essential that the consultant act with integrity, as failure to do so will result in questions being raised about why they are there in the first place, and, in extreme circumstances, result in the termination of the engagement and the non-payment of fees. And finally, demonstrating concern about the client, their organization and people is vital if the consultant is to be taken seriously, and not considered to be there for just the fees. Small things matter in this respect, as even picking up a book on the client's business is something that is greatly appreciated. Showing concern will also vary considerably within each of the four cultures.

I would challenge every consultant who reads this to look at Figure 8.1 and ask themselves whether they step up to the mark. Many I fear will fall at the first hurdle. And, for those that pass the first, the other two are likely to present major barriers to their earning trust. It is a shame that so many consultants do not really care for their clients, merely seeing them as a source of fee income. This is not the way to generate trust. I would also challenge any clients who happen to be reading this book to ask themselves if their consultants are meeting these three criteria. If they are not, it might be worth considering removing them and hiring some who do. If I was a client, I would also go one stage further and sit down with the account manager (or lead consultant if there isn't one) and ask them face to face if they believe they can really be trusted. I have come across clients who feel that they owe consultancies a living, preferring not to rock the boat when they are adding no value. It's time such clients took more control.

Relationship management extends across the complete consulting life cycle. It touches the account management process, how consultancy is sold and how it is delivered. As we saw in Chapter 1, consultancy is not purely about intelligence or selling in intelligent consultants to solve client problems. It has much more to do with the way consultants interact with their clients, which includes how they gain commitment, manage issues as they arise, and maintain productive working and professional relationships.

The basis of client relationships

Relationship management should achieve three things. First, it should develop insights into the client and its business, and apply these to the engagement and account management processes. Second, it should allow the consultancy to learn incrementally about the client, so that over time it knows more about the client and its business. Third, it should seek to develop selective relationships that are consensual and deep. This implies that the relationships with the client are long term rather than transactional and associated only with the current engagement. It also suggests that the role of the consultant in the client–consultant relationship should aim to become one of advisor and partner, rather than slave or servant. In the former a healthy and productive relationship is developed in which the client and consultant share concerns, issues and risks, as well as visions, plans and opportunities. This creates a shared understanding and allows the consultancy to anticipate and meet the real needs of the client. In the latter the relationship tends to be shallow, with the consultant being at the beck and call of the client, who has little regard for the additional value the consultant can bring to the relationship. Because excellent relationships depend on establishing and maintaining high levels of trust, we need to understand how trust is created.

David Maister talks about the following trust equation,[5] which consists of four elements: credibility, reliability, intimacy and self-orientation.

- *Credibility*: this is principally content-driven, and something that most consultants and consultancies spend considerable time honing through training, reading and absorbing experience from their engagements. This follows the arguments set out in Chapter 1, which suggested that consultants typically rely on their raw intelligence to get by. Because the link between credibility (technical expertise) and intelligence is strong, it should come as no surprise that most consultants would appear credible in their client's eyes. But there is more to credibility than just content. Real credibility requires that the client trusts the consultant in an emotional sense, which can only come from working with them. A curriculum vitae can display technical credibility, but it is only through working with the client that the consultant can generate the kind of credibility that translates into trust.
- *Reliability*: this is about delivering the consultancy in a consistent and reliable manner, and no client likes erratic or inconsistent delivery from any consultant or consultancy. Being seen to be reliable in the client's eyes will take time, and is strongly correlated with both how long you have known the client and how well the consultancy has been delivered. So, although the client will initially rely on your credibility (as demonstrated in your curriculum vitae) you will ultimately be assessed on your ability to deliver your promises. If over time this is effective and consistent, the client will perceive you to be reliable and trustworthy. Just with credibility, reliability also has an emotional element to it, and it is here where the cultural aspects come to the fore. This emotional element usually occurs when the engagement is executed in a way that the client finds satisfying. According to Maister, we form opinions about someone's reliability by the way they mirror our own habits, expectations, routines and so on. This is the client who openly states that it is pleasing to work with you because you think and act in a similar way. And, if carefully planned, a similar reaction can occur within an engagement. Using the cultural intelligence concept it is possible to prepare the engagement team so that it behaves in a way that the client will find appealing from a cultural sense. And by matching the client style very early on in the engagement it should be possible to establish its trust more rapidly. Thus, as we saw in Chapter 7, delivering the engagement will vary from one culture to another. This is equally true for relationship management.
- *Intimacy*: given the arrogance of most consultants, it is quite rare for intimate client–consultant relationships to develop. By intimate, I mean the ability to develop open and honest relationships in which the client can discuss difficult issues and problems they are having in their business, be they associated with internal or external events. Being intimate is often confused with client entertaining, and often leads to relationship managers spending their time wining and dining their clients. In reality, most clients view these events as a veiled attempt at selling rather than any genuine concern for the issues that frame their business. Many consultants shy away from intimacy because there is a risk associated with it, and it requires both parties to open themselves up to the other. Despite this, clients, especially those holding senior positions, value such intimacy with their consultants and are more willing to open up than their advisors. Being intimate therefore involves taking a genuine interest in the person(s) you are working with and taking the

trouble to understand what makes them tick. By the same token it means sharing some of your own values, ambitions and so forth.

- *Self-orientation*: in general, more value is placed on consultants who take a greater interest in their clients rather than in themselves. The problem is that most consultants are exceptionally egocentric and tend to be insensitive to the real concerns of their clients. What self-orientation actually means for consultants is a need to take more care in understanding their clients by listening more, being honest when they don't have an answer, by concentrating on defining the problem rather than jumping to a solution, and focusing wholly on the client.

Having discussed trust and the basis of client relationships we can now turn to probably one of the most important activities the consultancy must perform: creating the relationship management strategy for the client.

Creating the relationship management strategy

One of the early actions that consultants should take when working with their client is the drawing up of a relationship strategy. This strategy should identify either those people within the client organization who will need active management to ensure they remain committed to the engagement, or those with whom the consultancy wishes to have a long-term client–consultant relationship. As a rule of thumb, these latter people are likely to be those that have positions of power and authority within the client, rather than lower or middle management. Of course consultants should not ignore middle management, as these people wield sufficient power within the organization to sabotage the engagement. Managing client relationships is very similar to managing stakeholders within a project. And, in order to manage them, it is essential to understand them. Therefore it is necessary for the account, sales and engagement team to analyse the client and respond accordingly to what they find. This can be achieved through the following steps (Figure 8.2):[6]

1. Identify client stakeholders. This will entail identifying those people within the client that will have an interest in the consultancy engagement and/or who ought to be involved in the ongoing relationship with the consultancy. When identifying the stakeholders, their likely roles within the relationship should be considered. For example, people involved with the sale will include those who can influence the outcome, those who have the power of veto, those who will be involved in making the decision and those who hold the purse strings. When the engagement is live the number of client staff involved will naturally increase, as will the relationship management overhead. At this stage it is important that the account manager is engaged to ensure the wider relationship management needs of the firm are addressed. The role of the account manager in this instance is to help the team farm the client and to leverage other consultants into the engagement. They should become the focal point for the client and the team alike. And, although they will not be expected to manage all the relationships, they will need to know who is seeing whom, when this is happening, what is being discussed and, of course, what is being sold.
2. Gather information on stakeholders. As each stakeholder is identified, information about the person should be collected. In addition to a firm-wide relationship management strategy, it is important to consider each stakeholder individually. This helps to share the

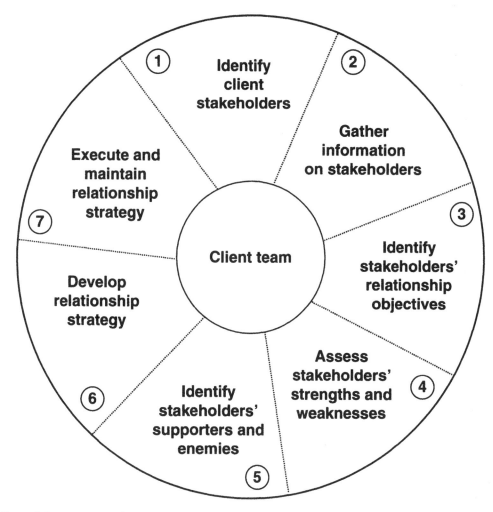

Figure 8.2   Developing the relationship management strategy

relationships across the consulting team and ensure the consultancy has exposure across as much of the client as possible. The types of information that should be collected include their role(s), responsibilities, position, their status and their sources of power (positional, status, knowledge, veto and expertise).

3. Identify all stakeholders' relationship objectives. This means understanding what the stakeholder and the firm want to achieve from the relationship. For many within the client's organization it will be a positive outcome from the consultancy engagement. But, recognizing that the engagement will result in a significant amount of turbulence, it is unlikely that this will be the case for all stakeholders. Therefore the strategy will need to reflect the nature of their feelings towards the engagement's outcomes. These should be tracked over time because stakeholders may well change their opinion about the engagement as it progresses. So, although some may view the engagement in a positive light to begin with, they may change their opinion as they realize what the outcome will mean for them personally (or their team, department or function). Any issues that arise from this will have to be addressed by the consultants on site. Equally important is to watch out for

those who appear ambivalent and sit on the fence. These people will often make their views known very late within the engagement, and if these are negative they can cause immense disruption. The consulting team should be aiming to smoke such people out as quickly as possible to ensure that the apparently neutral stakeholder's real feelings are known. The various stakeholders will also be looking for other outcomes, including opportunities for promotions, resolution of power struggles and a chance to gain knowledge from the consultants. Understanding these drivers is essential to the relationship strategy and will affect how each stakeholder is managed. The best way to understand this is to ask, as most clients will be willing to state what they want out of the relationship. In essence it is about establishing each stakeholder's WIIFM ('what's in it for me') and then working to meet it throughout the relationship. This stage is also about identifying what the consultancy wants to achieve from the relationships it will be establishing within the client. For the most part it will wish to develop a trusted advisor role. However, there will be instances where consultants will be seeking to position themselves to win a larger contract, and will therefore focus the short term on securing small assignments as a way of positioning themselves with the client. Once inside, the consultants will develop relationships with the decision-makers associated with the work the consultancy is really aiming to win. Ultimately the decision about the nature of the account relationship that the firm wishes to have resides with the account manager and senior executives/partners of the firm (see Chapter 5 for more details).

4. Assess stakeholders' strengths and weaknesses. The relationship strategy should take into account the relative strengths and weaknesses of each stakeholder. These can range from personal characteristics, such as emotional intelligence and persuasive ability, through to leadership characteristics, creditability, peer respect and so on. The purpose of this assessment is twofold. First, it is to identify the areas of weakness that may have to be covered by the consulting team, which is especially important when working at senior levels. Second, it is to watch out for areas of risk within the relationship in order to predict the issues and manage them appropriately.

5. Identify stakeholders' supporters and enemies. No one is an island, and it would be naïve to expect that everyone within the client will get on well with everyone else all of the time. As we saw in Chapter 7, power struggles and political manoeuvring are integral parts of any organization, and are usually exacerbated during consultancy engagements. The purpose of this stage of developing the strategy is to create a relationship map of the major links that exist between each of the identified stakeholders. Mapping these out will allow the consultants to identify the major groupings within the client, how they relate to each other and ultimately how they should be managed (Figure 8.3). It is also very useful to plot each stakeholder's position in relation to the engagement/consultancy (positive, negative or neutral). The example shown in Figure 8.3 suggests that the engagement team has access only to a small number of the stakeholders they need to manage. However, by mapping the relationships between the client staff it is possible to manage the relationship through one of the other stakeholders identified in the relationship map. In addition, it helps to understand how an individual stakeholder's opinion of the consultancy or engagement can be influenced by another. This stage will also help to clarify some of the political dimensions to the client that are likely to affect the engagement as it progresses. The arrows within Figure 8.3 represent the influence one stakeholder has over another, and the +ve, –ve and neutral indicators next to each stakeholder represent their feelings toward the engagement.

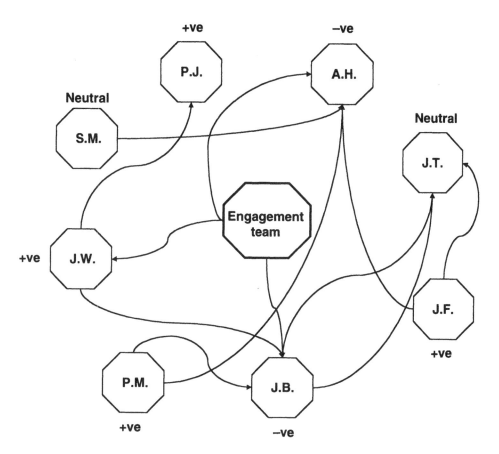

Figure 8.3 The relationship map

6. Develop the relationship strategy. This will bring everything together for each of the key relationships that are to be managed and for the client relationship as a whole. The strategy should describe how each relationship will be managed and by whom. It is very important to match the correct consultant to each client. In some cases it will be necessary to involve very senior consultants, whilst in others it will be possible to use more junior consultants. Although all consultants involved with the client should have some basic relationship management skills, some will require additional skills and position to be acceptable to the client. The relationship strategy will acknowledge this.

7. Execute and maintain the relationship strategy. Like everything else the strategy should never be set in stone, as there will be the inevitable staff changes both within the client and the consultancy. Moreover, there may be instances where the client and consultancy agree to roll off a consultant who may no longer be adding value or indeed may not fit in. Responding positively to such requests is very important.

It is often very useful to create a summary sheet for each of the major stakeholders (see Table 8.1 for a fictitious example) as this can be used as a ready source of intelligence across the account team and help new consultants as they join the engagement. Naturally, because some of the information contained within the stakeholder summary is sensitive it goes without saying that it shouldn't be left lying around.

Table 8.1 Relationship strategy summary

	Stakeholder summary
Engagement	Implementation of a new ERP system plus associated process and organizational change
Client	Acme Petrochemicals, subsidiary of Acme Conglomerates plc
Stakeholder	James Smith-Houston
Position	Chief information officer
Sources of power	Positional and expertise
Decision-maker role	Influencer, sponsor
Perception of engagement	Pro-engagement and pro the firm's role
WIIFM	Sees a successful ERP implementation as strengthening his position on the board
Other drivers	Seeks wider group IT role, ideally on Acme's board
Strengths	Very strong technologist, seen to be even-handed, and considered a good diplomat, generally well respected at board level
Weaknesses	Business knowledge is not as extensive as it could be, can fly off the handle, can be too technical at times
Supporters	Peter Quarts – CEO; James Smart – Group CFO
Enemies	Simon Peak – Group CIO; some parts of the business who see IT as failing to deliver robust systems
Strategy	Appoint Ian Woodman to work closely with James to develop the ERP and programme strategy. We as a firm need to ensure the implementation runs smoothly, as this will position us well with James and the Petrochemicals Board. It is known that there are some wider opportunities at Group, and this engagement will give us suitable exposure and position the firm well with the main board.

The cultural dimensions to relationship management

From a cultural perspective, relationship management has a national and organizational dimension to it. Within the national dimension of culture it is worth considering how important trust is to fostering effective relationships. Francis Fukuyama in his book *Trust*[7] makes the distinction between low and high trust societies. In low trust societies, organizations tend to be family based, with trust limited to the confines of the extended family (the immediate family plus aunts, uncles and so on). This is typical of China, southern Italy and North Africa. For the consultant working within these countries it is essential to be accepted, and hence trusted by the family. Once this happens other opportunities beyond the immediate client tend to present themselves. This is because within such societies, a small number of powerful families will dominate commercial and government organizations. I experienced this whilst working in the Sudan, where the client had links to the government and other commercial organizations. Through these we were able to explore other consulting opportunities that would not have been possible had we failed to win the trust of the client. In contrast to such familistic societies are those that have a high degree of what Fukuyama terms generalized social trust. Germany, Japan and the United States fall into this category. Here private sector firms tend to be much larger. Such countries may not in themselves be high trust, but what they do possess is a system of formal rules and regulations, which have to be agreed, administered by law and enforced. However, earning trust within such countries will vary. For example, within Germany trust is placed in those that have the academic and professional qualifications to execute their job. Therefore a focus on technical and intellectual status, backed up by qualifications, tends to win trust more readily. Another aspect worth addressing when working internationally is the use of language.[8] Although in general people will use a mixture of oral and written communication, the proportions will vary according to culture. It is important for the consultant to know what the preference is, as this will influence how trustworthy they are perceived to be by the client. For example, when dealing with those cultures that prefer a written communication style (countries in north-west Europe and the Americas) it is better to keep a formal written record, as these cultures do not take the spoken word seriously. The converse is true within those cultures that prefer the oral form (south-west Europe, China and Asia-Pacific countries), as here the written word is considered less important than the spoken word. Indeed, in some cases emphasizing the importance of the written word can cause problems, as the following example from the management writer Charles Handy illustrates:[9]

> I remember my first exposure to the 'Chinese contract'. I was a manager in South Malaysia for an oil company, responsible amongst other things for negotiating agency agreements with our Chinese dealers. I was young, enthusiastic and, I suppose, naïve. After the conclusion of one such negotiation, the dealer and I shook hands, drank the ritual cups of tea, and were, I felt, the best of friends. I took the official company agency agreement out of my case and started to fill in the figures, preparatory to signing it. 'Why are you doing that?' asked the dealer in some alarm. 'If you think that I am going to sign that you are much mistaken.' 'But I am only writing in the figures which we agreed.' 'If we agreed them, why do you want a legal document? It makes me suspect that you have got more out of this agreement than I have, and are going to use the weight of law to enforce your terms. In my culture,' he went on, 'a good agreement is self-enforcing because both parties go away smiling and are happy to see that each of us is smiling. If one smiles and the other scowls, the agreement will not stick, lawyers or no lawyers.'

When considering the international dimensions of culture with regard to relationships it is also worth remembering the four dimensions of international cultures described by Hofstede: power distance, individualism–collectivism, masculinity–femininity and uncertainty avoidance (Chapter 2). These too will have a bearing on how the relationship between client and consultant should work.

Relationship management in the four cultures

As expected, the nature and form of client relationships within each of the four cultures will vary. This will reflect the way things work within each of the four cultures and how the consultancy earns the trust of its client. It also requires that the consultancy considers very carefully the nature of power within each of the four cultures and plays to it in order to achieve its relationship objectives. And, although this is distinct from the politics of the engagement (see Chapter 7), the two are closely linked. As we discussed in the last chapter, Robert Greene has described 48 laws of power[10] which manifest themselves within organizations and people's behaviour. I will not replicate these here, but I will include those that are relevant to each of the four cultures as I describe how the relationship management process should work within each. For completeness, I will include the law's number for those who wish to investigate further.

NETWORKED – FRIENDSHIP

Relationship management within the networked culture is based upon establishing friends across the organization. This requires the consultant to take deliberate actions to meet key people within the client, some of whom will not be directly associated with the engagement. This latter point is important, as it serves two purposes. First, it allows information about the engagement to be spread across the organization, itself an essential aspect in establishing and maintaining commitment. Second, it begins to create a strong brand image of the consultancy in other parts of the organization. If the engagement is perceived to be successful, then this widening of the consultancy relationship should allow further opportunities to be identified and new work sold. Because the networked culture is strong on sociability, it is necessary to take a genuine interest in every client contact's personal life. Of all the four cultures it is the networked that is concerned the most about what happens outside work, probably more than what happens inside. Therefore, socializing with key members of the client team is usually acceptable, and client entertaining is one way in which to enhance the relationship. Although the networked culture is not a strongly political one, or one in which power is overtly displayed, it is important to play to the relevant power laws, as this will create a perception of power around the consultant. The following laws should be obeyed:

- Law 13: *when asking for help, appeal to people's self-interest, never to their mercy or gratitude.* This plays to the WIIFM identified during the stakeholder analysis and also the nature of the networked culture. Therefore, in all relationships it is important to seek out every contact's WIIFM, even if it means asking.
- Law 18: *do not build fortresses to protect yourself – isolation is dangerous.* No one is an island, and this is particularly the case within the networked culture. Appearing isolated will be considered counter-cultural and it will cut the consultant off from the rest of the client. A much better strategy is to make friends around the organization, as this will provide a ready source of information about the current engagement and future opportunities.
- Law 43: *work on the hearts and minds of others.* Coercion does not work within the networked culture, and if used it will ultimately work against the consultant. Winning the hearts and minds of the client during the engagement is essential if you are to be accepted.

COMMUNAL – PASSION

Successful relationships within the communal culture rely on displaying a combination of passion and focus. This means that becoming part of the client's family is the most important aspect of the relationship management process, and will involve the consultant's committing to becoming involved with the client outside work. Committing to the client's credo is essential. And giving your all to the client and its mission will be well received. Furthermore, making yourself useful beyond the immediate assignment will endear you to those you come into contact with, and will demonstrate commitment. Of the four cultures, it is the communal that is the most fun for the consultant. Even though relationships are likely to be intensive, the combination of passion and self-belief with the focus on getting the job done makes for one of those rare moments in consultancy – excitement. Power is dispersed within the communal culture, and as such the power laws that apply here are mainly associated with creating a general impression of you and the firm. Therefore, adhere to the following:

- Law 6: *court attention at all costs*. Because of the self-belief and passionate nature of the communal culture, it is necessary to take on a larger-than-life persona – fading into the background like a grey man will ensure a short shelf-life. Instead become the centre of attention as much as you can, leading change, being the life and soul of the party and so on.
- Law 28: *enter action with boldness*. Taking bold actions is part and parcel of the communal culture. Therefore, it is vital that actions are committed to without hesitation. And remember that failure is acceptable as long as you learn from it.

MERCENARY – POWER

The sheer focus on getting the job done at all costs creates a strong focus on power within the mercenary culture. And because it is a dog-eat-dog environment the relationship management strategy should focus on matching powerful consultants (either intellectually or positionally) to key clients. Mercenary cultures prefer to have strong-willed consultants because the relationship typically involves a lot of conflict. And because the client is usually very arrogant there is a need to have very self-confident consultants on site. People who are not used to the political and power plays that occur within the mercenary culture are unlikely to survive that long. When developing the relationship strategy it is also necessary to consider how the power plays will pan out over time. Because it is rare that people remain in power too long (mainly because they make too many enemies on the way up the organization) it is important to identify alternative sources of power and develop relationships with them as well. In this way the consultants will insulate themselves from any fallout that would arise from the loss of a powerful sponsor. Because everything is work-focused, socializing with the client tends to be rare and is typically associated with the completion of a project or other major event. Mercenary cultures are not safe places. It is rare to gain the same levels of intimacy within the mercenary culture as in either the networked or communal organization. The relevant power laws within the mercenary culture are as follows:

- Law 2: *never put too much trust in friends – learn how to use enemies*. This may sound devious, but in the mercenary organization it is very important to know both who the enemies are and how to win them over. Because of the political nature of mercenary organizations it is often necessary to appear to be on everyone's side, as this is a sure way of protecting yourself against the inevitable crossfire.

- Law 9: *win through your actions, never through argument.* Because mercenary cultures are action-oriented they tend to dismiss rhetoric. As a consultant there is little value in talking about what needs to be done, it is important to just do it. Demonstrating by doing will not only lead to a rapid acceptance by the client, it will also increase the reputation and power for you and the firm.
- Law 15: *crush your enemy totally* (metaphorically of course). Never underestimate what people will do to get their own way within mercenary cultures. The stakeholder analysis should focus on those who will be out to sabotage the engagement and/or the relationship, and how the threat they pose can be eliminated. It should be clear why relationships within the mercenary culture need to be at a sufficiently high level, as it is only those in power who can really make things happen.

FRAGMENTED – COMPETENCE

The fragmented culture is probably the most difficult and least fun to work in, and the hardest to create relationships within. This is because most people dislike and mistrust each other, and this is no different for the consultant. Publicly staff in the client will appear to be convivial and friendly, but behind closed doors the opposite is true. The use of the stakeholder mapping technique described in this chapter is especially useful within the fragmented organization, as you will need to be on your guard with everyone you come into contact with. The map, once completed, should be used to pinpoint those people within the client the firm needs to establish a relationship with. When developing the relationship find out how you can add personal value – if you scratch their back, they are likely to scratch yours.

There is very little socializing within the fragmented organization because there is no friendship, so don't expect to be attending any large social events. However, do expect to have the odd drink or meal with your direct client, and use these to gather intelligence about what's going on in their organization. Because the fragmented culture is politically sophisticated, power will be wielded in subtle ways. As a relationship builder you will need to be equally subtle in your use of power. As a result, the relevant power laws are more numerous than in the other cultures and most have a political edge to them:

- Law 3: *conceal your intentions.* Getting things done within the fragmented culture means that it is often necessary to prepare a course of action very carefully by hiding your true intentions. Playing members of the client off against each other to meet a broader objective has to be achieved without anyone suspecting you are behind it. This requires guile and tact.
- Law 14: *pose as a friend, work as a spy.* Playing the spy is an essential part of law 3. Selectively passing intelligence to your contacts across the organization is a key method to keep people on your side. But this has to be carried out in a friendly and seemingly innocent way. It is rare that you will be found out, as people within fragmented cultures rarely see the bigger picture.
- Law 19: *know who you're dealing with – never offend the wrong person.* This is very important within the fragmented organization, as unlike the mercenary culture where power is obvious, here it is more diluted. The stakeholder map will allow you to identify those you must not offend.
- Law 20: *do not commit to anyone.* Part of the art of relationship building within fragmented cultures is the ability not to take sides. Commitment in this case refers to taking sides in

arguments, not committing to complete the assignment or help the client. Getting caught in political crossfire is a very real danger and so it is important to appear to be even-handed, playing to both sides.

- Law 24: *play the perfect courtier*. This really sums up the nature of relationships for this type of client. Acting in a way that flatters, yields when necessary and asserts power in an oblique way is central to successful relationships.

Table 8.2 summarizes the key points for relationships within each of the four cultures.

Table 8.2   Relationship management in the four cultures

Networked	Communal	Mercenary	Fragmented
• Map the organization in terms of a relationship network • Identify the major groupings within the organization and manage them accordingly • Understand how you can gain access to the major players through those within your network • Do not become a fortress: make sure you have a strong client network • Win the hearts and minds of the client's staff	• Join the family inside and outside work • Make yourself useful to everyone by taking whatever actions are necessary • Be the centre of attention, displaying energy and enthusiasm • Be bold in your actions: committing to a course of action is far better than holding back • Be prepared to fail; taking risks is acceptable	• Seek out how you can create a winning opportunity for each client contact • Don't expect much socializing • Identify, work with and influence those in power • Arguments are won through actions – don't bother with words, they count for little • Never trust people totally: the nature of power will inevitably shift, and you will have to shift with it	• Identify the important relationships and make sure you don't offend the wrong people • Accept that no one trusts each other • Don't expect any socializing • Play the perfect courtier and use tact and guile to secure favour

---

THE CULTURALLY INTELLIGENT RELATIONSHIP MANAGER

- understands the basic cultural differences of the four client cultures and what this means for the relationship management strategy
- develops a strategy that meets the needs of the firm and the client culture
- recognizes that power will be wielded differently within each of the four cultures
- will obey the relevant power laws for each culture
- remembers that relationship management boils down to developing trust.

Summary

Relationship management is an art. It is central to the delivery of the engagement and the account management process. Client relationships must be deeply embedded within the distribution of power across the organization. This means that the consultant must understand and work within the power laws applicable to the client culture. Whenever in any doubt as to the purpose of relationship management see Figure 8.1 – it's all about trust.

III Creating the culturally intelligent firm

Questionnaire – How culturally aligned is *your* firm?

Answer the following questions by choosing the option that is the closest to your normal response. No multiple answers are allowed. I have deliberately avoided the catch-all answer, as it is too easy to opt for the 'all of the above' response and does not force the issue of what is most important to you in a given situation. When answering think about how you behave now, rather than how you ought to behave. The results will provide you with an indication of the level of cultural intelligence that currently resides within your firm. It will also establish the baseline from which you can develop the necessary cultural sophistication using the model and techniques described in this book. If you are tackling this questionnaire before starting the book, I recommend you repeat the exercise once you have completed Parts I and II, but this time take a view of where you ought to be rather than where you are now.

1. You have just won a major engagement with a client that operates in the United States, Europe and Asia-Pacific. Do you:
(a) mobilize your team and send them off as soon as possible with only the minimum of preparation – after all they are smart enough to cope, aren't they?
(b) decide to source the team from your staff in the relevant countries because they will know more about the local culture and working practices that will affect the engagement?
(c) bring together the best team of technical experts and brief them on the working environments in each country and then mobilize them?

2. One of your consultants has been asked to leave a client. Do you:
(a) accept that these things happen from time to time and attempt to get another consultant on site as soon as possible?
(b) meet the client to get to the bottom of the issue and feed this back to the consultant?
(c) discuss the issue with the consultant to understand their perspective and view this as personal development?
(d) use feedback from the client and consultant to update your client–consultant processes, especially in relation to how you prepare your staff before they start work with this and other clients?

3. Your induction course for new consultants majors on:
(a) the history of your firm
(b) basic procedures and processes (time recording, expense policy and so on)
(c) what it means to be client-intimate and the implications this has for the way your staff are expected to work with your clients.

4. When recruiting client-facing staff, what is the overriding factor when deciding whether to accept the candidate?
(a) technical skills, as these indicate how saleable they will be with your clients
(b) interpersonal skills, as these determine how well they will fit with your team
(c) intrapersonal skills, as these show how stable and resilient the candidate is
(d) client-handling skills, as these allow you to assess how well they can manage relationships
(e) cultural sensitivity displayed by cross-sector and international experience, as this will indicate their ability to adjust to different client contexts and cultures.

5. You are meeting a prospective client for the first time: what is the most important thing to attempt to find out?
(a) the current state of its business
(b) the problems or opportunities it needs to attend to
(c) its previous experience of consultants (good and bad)
(d) what its culture is
(e) what it would expect of your firm when you work with it.

6. You have a new consultancy proposition: how do you take it to market?
(a) produce glossy brochures and send them to all your clients
(b) develop a standard process around it so that it can be delivered in a consistent way, irrespective of your clients
(c) discuss the proposition with your clients to understand how it can be tailored to make it work for them.

7. When developing a proposal do you usually:
(a) concentrate on the technical dimensions of the solution?
(b) describe in detail the process through which the solution will be implemented?
(c) ensure the solution is presented in a way that matches the client's preferred working style/culture?

8. You are selecting a new account manager for one of your key accounts. What is the dominant factor that determines your choice?
(a) industry knowledge
(b) sales expertise
(c) relationship management skills
(d) previous experience of the client
(e) whoever is available.

9. When making your sales presentation to the client do you:
(a) follow a set pattern?
(b) focus on those things that the client will be particularly interested in?

10. You are pulling your engagement team together following a big sales win. Do you:
(a) choose whoever is not currently on assignment?
(b) select the team on the basis of technical and industry skills?
(c) select the team on the basis of their interpersonal and relationship-building skills?
(d) select the team on the basis of their ability to work in the client's culture?

11. When preparing your engagement team do you:
(a) leave it to the team to work things out?
(b) develop detailed work-package descriptions and assignment objectives?
(c) provide the team with a brief about the engagement and how to work with the client, including the behaviours that are valued and those that should be avoided?

12. Where is most of your staff development and training directed?
(a) technical skills, focused on whatever the market wants now and those skills that might be needed in the future

(b) interpersonal skills, such as relationship management
(c) intrapersonal skills that will help your consultants become more self-aware and high-performing
(d) cultural skills that will help them work with different clients both internationally and organizationally.

13. When you have won or lost a sale do you:
(a) move on without analysing why you won/lost?
(b) ask the client why they chose/rejected you?
(c) analyse the win/loss taking into account client and firm input and placing the win/loss in the context of all your other sales outcomes to establish patterns?

14. When structuring your engagement do you:
(a) decide on how it should be structured before starting?
(b) work with the client to ensure it is structured to be successful within its environment?

15. When appraising your staff at the end of the year, which is the most important?
(a) the hard elements, such as sales and utilization
(b) 360 degree feedback from peers, subordinates and managers
(c) client feedback.

ANSWERS

1.	(a) 1	(b) 3	(c) 3		
2.	(a) 1	(b) 2	(c) 2	(d) 3	
3.	(a) 1	(b) 1	(c) 3		
4.	(a) 2	(b) 2	(c) 2	(d) 3	(e) 3
5.	(a) 2	(b) 2	(c) 3	(d) 3	(e) 4
6.	(a) 1	(b) 2	(c) 3		
7.	(a) 1	(b) 1	(c) 3		
8.	(a) 2	(b) 2	(c) 2	(d) 2	(e) –3
9.	(a) 1	(b) 3			
10.	(a) 0	(b) 2	(c) 2	(d) 3	
11.	(a) 0	(b) 1	(c) 3		
12.	(a) 1	(b) 2	(c) 3	(d) 3	
13.	(a) 0	(b) 2	(c) 3		
14.	(a) 1	(b) 3			
15.	(a) 1	(b) 2	(c) 3.		

HOW DID YOU FARE?

Your score is not an absolute measure of your firm's cultural intelligence, as that is something that cannot be measured precisely. However, what it does give you is an indication of how sensitive you are to the factors that make your clients unique and a general reflection of how much effort you spend getting intimate with them. It also shows where your usual focus lies. It is possible to score a maximum of 45 points, although I would be suspicious of anyone scoring this highly.

If your score is less than 15 then you have a lot to do. With so little cultural intelligence it is probably by luck that you are successful, if indeed you are. It's about time that you started to take more care of your clients by understanding their agenda and ways of working in more detail. Your likely model of consultancy is one that is based upon technical expertise in which you know best for your client, rather than establishing its true agenda and working hard to deliver it. Transactional rather than relationship-based consulting is the preferred intervention style. I would not be surprised if your clients found you arrogant and uncaring, and felt that your fee earners looked down on them. Some clients may love you, but the majority will put up with you and some may even kick you out. Repeat business is limited. Of course, this is an extreme view, but there are some consultancies that believe that the client should be honoured to have them on board, rather than the other way around. It is time to take action, and advance your firm's skills in client handling and delivery on the basis of understanding what makes your client tick. Who knows, you may find that it increases your revenue, reduces your cost of sales and allows you to do more interesting work.

If you have scored between 15 and 30, you have some basic understanding of cultural intelligence. Yours is probably one of the majority of firms that have some switched-on staff who are adept at adjusting when they move from one client to another. The problem here is that these skills have almost invariably been learned from experience and self-learning, and are likely to be restricted to a small number of fee earners. In essence they are intuitive not deliberate. Clients are generally satisfied and relationships are pretty good. However, there will be a few occasions when there is a major clash between yourself and your client, and some of your staff may find it problematic moving from client to client. Because these skills are intuitive, they are not shared amongst the fee earners and hence the success will be down to individuals, which can make it difficult for you when resourcing jobs. The key action here is to harness the latent cultural intelligence that resides within pockets across the firm and make it a collective skill. This can be achieved through training, mentoring and coaching.

If your score is greater than 30 and you have answered the questionnaire honestly then your firm has a genuinely strong sense of cultural intelligence. You may even have worked this out for yourself and have developed the processes, feedback loops and knowledge management tools to share this skill across the firm. If this is the case you will probably have a recruitment process that allows you to select staff that fit your modus operandi. However, unless you have a solid understanding of, or interest in, culture, your cultural intelligence is probably based upon a combination of sector understanding and intuition, which makes it less hit-and-miss than those firms that scored 15–30, but it is still inconsistently applied. You probably know that most investment banks behave in a similar way, as do manufacturers and retail organizations. What you don't have is a means of distilling the underlying cultural attributes that allow you and your consultants to develop the necessary consistency of approach and which facilitate the smooth transition from one client to the next. As with those firms that scored 15–30 you still have room for improvement. Ensuring that every consultant has a basic level of cultural intelligence will allow you to raise your game even further.

Part III is designed to round off the topic of cultural intelligence by focusing on the firm rather than the core consulting processes or the individual. It begins by looking at the issue of competitive advantage in consultancy (Chapter 9) and how cultural intelligence can be used to achieve it. Chapter 10 describes how firms can develop and sustain high levels of cultural intelligence by updating their internal processes, including recruitment and induction. At the end of Part III I have included a recommended reading list that details a number of texts that will allow readers to enhance their consulting skills.

9 *Cultural intelligence and competitive advantage*

Market leadership is increasingly hard to win – and even harder to keep. Customers are more demanding and less loyal than ever before, yet many markets are so saturated that the customer finds it impossible to distinguish between one 'me-too' product and another.[1]

It is not enough if the buyer obtains great service by catching the right senior professional on a good day. Brand value is created if – and only if – certain standards of performance are obtained every time the buyer uses the firm. To a very real extent, therefore, a firm name (and hence a firm) will have value to the extent that it has procedures to enforce its quality standards.[2]

Which is it to be? Operationally excellent, product leading or customer intimate

Michael Treacy and Fred Wiersema, authors of *The discipline of market leaders*, provide some important perspectives on the way market-leading firms are focused and how they distinguish themselves from their competition. These views are particularly relevant to consultancies because there is little that separates one consultancy from another. Indeed from an initial scan of the market, most appear to offer the same products and services, and all purport to have recruited the best brains available. Of course, not every firm can have the best of the best, and this helps to create some market distinction between, for example, the top-tier and second-tier firms. Consultancies, like any other company, will fall into one of the three camps identified by Treacy and Wiersema. They can choose to focus on operational excellence, product leadership or customer intimacy.

Operationally excellent consultancies are not product or service innovators, nor are they interested in forging deep client relationships. Such firms field staff who behave identically and deliver their craft in the same way irrespective of the client or the engagement. They train their staff to follow a consistent method and tool kit without any regard for individuality or flair. Unsurprisingly their induction process is rigorous, consistent and unvarying. Also, as long as the consulting processes and methods followed are best in class and applied consistently they can guarantee success most of the time. The culture is defined by process and procedure, and by the ability to indoctrinate new joiners as rapidly as possible. This ensures that within a short space of time all new hires display consistent behaviours that are congruent with the culture of the firm. Operationally excellent consultancies run themselves like a military operation, with the team overriding the individual – free spirits are not generally welcome, and in any case are often weeded out during the selection process. Everyone knows the rule book and the processes that matter. They will deliver their work according to both. The bottom line for these consultancies is that they deliver a swift, dependable service. The problem with this model is that it sometimes loses sight of the client and its sensitivities. This is because consultancies become obsessed with process and substituting client staff for their own (whom they know and have trained to deliver a consistent product). A good example of this type of consultancy is Accenture, which has developed a consistency in service and staff that few of the other consultancies can match.

Product-leading consultancies offer their customers best-of-breed products and innovation. These are the firms that develop new concepts, prepare the market through thought leadership and deliver their service in a product-centric way. Unlike the operationally excellent consultancy, they recruit people with technical expertise and product-development skills, and expect them to continue to push the boundaries of the firm. Product-excellent consultancies are not driven by procedure but by talented individuals capable of generating new ideas and concepts, time and time again. Managing the people in these firms involves real talent management, from recruitment through to growing, guiding and retaining the most valuable staff. This means that unthinking clones are not welcome, but mavericks and inspirational and unconventional people are (although the whole firm cannot be full of such individuals). Establishing a standard method that applies to all products and services is less important, because each product will require a separate set of tools and processes to deliver it. Of course, products do not sell themselves so it is essential that the market is cultivated to prepare and educate their clients. This involves using thought-leadership avenues such as articles (in journals such as the *Harvard Business Review*), writing and publishing books that introduce new concepts, and speaking on the lecture circuit. These companies are expert at the product launch. Because there are potentially thousands of ideas that can be pursued, the product-leading consultancy will be smart at the way it narrows the field down to a few killer products and service lines, and the way it then places its best brains to work up the proposition into something that will sell. A good example of a product-leading consultancy would be Computer Science Corporation, whose work on re-engineering the corporation set off the business process re-engineering revolution.

Customer-intimate consultancies focus on delivering not what the market wants but what specific customers need. More importantly, such firms deliberately seek to cultivate relationships rather than pursue transactions. They are specialists in satisfying their customer's unique needs, and achieve this by being close to them and developing a deep understanding of their organization. Customer-intimate firms personalize their basic service and products to meet client requirements. The basic building blocks remain the same, but the end product is tailored. Interestingly, such companies are more willing to take risks on behalf of their clients in order to meet their needs. Customer-intimate firms do not seek out the latest product or service innovation, nor do they subscribe to the one best way of delivery. Instead they provide products and services to clients that are based upon their deep understanding of their business. This not only recognizes that new ideas, concepts, products and services can be developed and disseminated much faster than ever before, but also that delivering change is much harder and more complex than it was ten years ago. The customer-intimate firm is one in which you will find no clones or androids – instead you will find a loose collection of individuals who bring a unique blend of skills, attitudes and behaviours in order to get the job done. This normally means that the firm recruits a combination of experienced consultants and innovative thinkers, which prevents the skills required to remain customer-intimate from becoming stale. As to be expected with such firms, customers themselves often become part of the process of remaining at the forefront of thinking. Interestingly, customer-intimate organizations only opt to work for clients who take the long view and with which they can develop long-lasting relationships. As a result they generally shun the transactional client. Although the firm may view this as being the right thing to do, we have seen in Chapter 6 that mercenary and fragmented cultures prefer the transactional arrangement. Therefore, this stance is probably unrealistic most of the time. The important thing is to recognize that being customer-intimate means adjusting to the needs and style of the client. Thus, in the transactional sales/engagement scenario the customer-intimate consultancy is still capable of showing how well it knows the client. Being transactional with those clients that prefer it will be perceived as being customer-intimate. Ernst & Young used to fall into this category prior to the sale of its management consultancy services division to Cap Gemini in May 2000.

Many firms attempt to be customer-intimate by simultaneously being product leaders and operationally excellent. Unfortunately this leads to a proliferation of products and inconsistent delivery. This is because in order to meet the perceived and actual client needs, new products and service lines spring up everywhere without any overall guidance on what products and services are actually required. As a result, the majority of consultants do not have a sufficiently detailed knowledge of the product or service to either sell it or apply it within their clients. This tends to lead to the emergence of product fiefdoms across the firm that meet local client needs but which fail to develop the consistency required to deliver them to all clients (assuming they needed it in the first place).

The importance of brand to the professional firm

Given the difficulty in distinguishing one firm from another, how can individual consultancies stand out from the ever-crowded market place? Consulting bodies and journals often publish league tables that show total fee income for the top 100 firms and revenue per sector for the top 30 or so firms. All this shows is how much fee income is earned, not how well services are delivered or how deep the client relationships are. Of course there are those consultancies that are more focused in certain sectors and technologies than others, and it might be assumed that this helps in setting them apart. But when there are a large number of these and hence plenty of choice, it is difficult to see how their technological or sectorial emphasis is really capable of making them stand out from the competition, especially over the longer term. Branding of professional firms is therefore becoming increasingly important.

In the general sense, branding is useful because it creates associations and hence a desire within the client organization, to purchase a particular product or service. If we were to look across the consulting landscape we would see a small number of firms that already have a brand image. For example, if anyone were to think of the major firms within the strategic consulting field, two would automatically come to mind: McKinsey and Boston Consulting Group. Both firms have very strong brand associations. These have developed through the specialist nature of their work (strategy not delivery), the length of time they have been providing their services and their ability to create consistency in, amongst others, the selection, training and development of their fee earners. Similarly, the Big Five management consultancies also tend to be well known because of their sheer size and global presence. This is reinforced by the links with their auditing practices that have a ready-made route to market (although, as we saw in the Introduction, these links are under increasing scrutiny from the SEC). They too have a well-trodden path of induction. All of this provides distinct market advantages over the mid-ranking and smaller firms, even though they are considerably more expensive. This combination works in their favour for most of the time. For example, the Big Five are often invited to respond to competitive bids without having to seek them out. Of course, it does not automatically mean that they will win the work, especially if the client is price-sensitive. However, there are some circumstances where one of the large consultancies is asked to work for the client in a non-competitive bid situation. This is where brand recognition comes into its own. Such situations also have a lot to do with a client's favoured consultancy and their association with them, either as clients or as former staff members. Indeed, some large firms take this latter point seriously, creating alumni of past members of the firm, which becomes an additional route to market. The real difficulty for the smaller consultancies is that they have to work hard at establishing brand recognition in a market place that is dominated by the large firms. To overcome this, smaller firms often focus on a single sector or a very small client base. Only once they have an established revenue stream will they expand into other clients and markets. Of course if the smaller firm is able to offer a combination of strong delivery and lower fees then it can be in a very strong position to win work when pitching against the larger firms. Small firms also have to contend with the size issue in other ways too. Because they are small, they do not have the resources available to deliver large engagements. In this case, having a network of professionals or other smaller firms is one way to get over this type of problem because it creates the perception of a much larger firm. Unsurprisingly there is an increasing trend within the smaller consultancy community of having a core number of staff and a network of associates and other smaller firms that can come together to work on large-scale engagements.

Branding is particularly important when there is an economic slump, because every firm is capable of competing on price. And as soon as one firm drops its fees, others will follow. Indeed, as we have seen from the Internet retailers, there will always be someone else who can undercut your fees. This often stores up problems for later when the recovery begins and firms attempt to raise prices. Unfortunately the clients, who have become accustomed to the cheaper rates, balk at any increase. A better strategy is to demonstrate the additional value provided by the firm is worth the higher fee.

In general, brand loyalty is decreasing because of the increasing information about alternatives. This is also the case with consultancy because there are many more consultancies than there were 10–15 years ago, and a number of the services have become commoditized (for example project management). With a growing number of smaller consultancies, either specializing in particular business areas or replicating the skills of the larger consultancies (but much more cheaply), clients have a broader range from which to select their consulting partners. The question this raises is how can clients differentiate between their consultancy suppliers, apart from the obvious factor of price? This takes us to the concept of brand as organization. This suggests that, unlike a product such as a Mars Bar or a bottle of Coca-Cola, which has immediate brand associations reinforced by advertising, consultancies do not have a tangible product to offer. Instead they have a bunch of intelligent people who can solve business problems. There is no 'product' in the simplistic sense, so branding has to be achieved through the process of delivery and relationship management. This implies that the firm has to ensure that its clients walk away from every engagement with a warm feeling and a desire to come back to the consultancy when it needs more help. To do this requires the consultancy to develop consistency in its fee-earning staff, both in terms of their attitudes and behaviours but also in the way in which they deliver the service. This is not easy. The problem that most firms face is that although each of its consultants is an ambassador for the firm, and it is they who collectively create the brand image with the clients, establishing consistency in style and delivery is actually quite hard. Basing the brand identity on the organization itself is a smart way to achieve market distinction. To achieve this requires the consulting firm to generate a well-communicated and clearly understood set of values, along with a consistent culture. This may be very difficult for the largest firms with their vast array of people, products and services. However, how else can they set themselves apart from their competitors? After all, every large firm states that it has the best professional staff, the best service-delivery record and the best skills required to make its clients successful. In reality this cannot be true in all cases. However, giving the impression that it is the best, and instilling a brand association with its clients that it is, is an effective way to capture and retain customers. Such things as perceived quality, innovation, customer concern and so on are some of the many associations that consultancies can generate. At its basic level branding gets you through the client's door and it allows you to commence the relationship. It then boils down to how well and how consistently the service is delivered. And if engagements are delivered to consistently high standards and receive great client feedback, a brand association of quality and effectiveness is established. It is this that really counts in consultancy (see Chapter 8 and the need to generate trust). This is where cultural intelligence comes in.

Cultural intelligence and competitive advantage

I believe that every capable consultant and consultancy must be genuinely concerned about their clients. Not from a fee-income perspective though, but from one that adds value and helps solve client problems. A customer-intimate strategy is essential if this is to work. It follows therefore that cultural intelligence when combined with all the other skills that a consultant should possess provides the basis for this intimacy. It cannot be superficial or some passing fad that allows you to secure more fees. Instead it must be an ethos that is embedded in the way accounts are established and grown, the way in which engagements are sold and delivered, and the way relationships are built. But before we get too carried away with this, we have to remember what customer intimacy is. It means getting under the skin of the client to the extent that you know what it needs and how it should be delivered.

Taken seriously, cultural intelligence provides the basis of competitive advantage for those consultancies that take its philosophy to heart. As we have seen it can be used to enhance the primary consultancy processes. The philosophy can be applied to any firm, irrespective of its size, although it should be simpler for the smaller firm. In summary, cultural intelligence provides competitive advantage by:

- allowing the consultancy to focus its sales and delivery on selective cultures
- improving the ratio of wins to losses across all four cultures, or those the firm selects to consult within
- minimizing the trauma caused when clients and consultants come together for the first time
- increasing the likelihood of client satisfaction by acting in a way that the customer can recognize
- reducing the probability of consultants (or the team) being asked to leave the client
- ensuring that relationships are managed in a way that suits the client.

Chapters 5, 6, 7 and 8 have described in detail how consultancy can be applied to the four consulting processes. The final chapter of the book looks at the internal processes and changes that need to be made to ensure the firm can become culturally intelligent.

10 *Creating and sustaining the culturally intelligent consultancy*

Throughout this book, I have discussed what cultural intelligence means in both a general and specific sense. What I have not done so far is detail how a culturally intelligent consulting firm can be created and sustained. This is the purpose of this final chapter. In addressing this I will also outline how two of the biggest problems associated with consultancy, making the results stick and going native, can be addressed through the application of cultural intelligence.

Establishing the culturally intelligent firm

BEGIN BY BENCHMARKING YOUR FIRM

The starting point for any firm is to benchmark itself with respect to its degree of cultural intelligence. There are three ways in which the consultancy can do this:

- qualitatively, by completing the questionnaire at the beginning of Part III
- quantitatively, by analysing sales data and clients to date using the process described in Chapter 5
- perceptively, through client feedback. Asking your clients why they use your firm can be insightful, especially if they are allowed to be candid. Most consultancies and especially the largest actively seek out client feedback on the completion of major engagements. This usually involves asking questions about the conduct of the team, value for money and whether the client would use the firm again in the future. Few ask clients what they actually liked about the firm. If asked the majority would mention that they liked their style or that the consultants blended in with their staff. This can be loosely interpreted as being culturally intelligent. It is well worth exploring this with the client – ideally face to face because it is a great way to see just how culturally intelligent your firm is.

NEXT, SET IN MOTION A SERIES OF ACTIONS

The results of the benchmarking exercise should feed into changes that should be made to the firm. Clearly, if you turn out to be very poor in relation to all three dimensions then you have a lot to do. But even where you perform well across all three, there is always room for improvement because it is probable that cultural intelligence will not be widespread, and is likely to be an intuitive skill rather than something that is deliberately instilled and embedded within your staff. The process of developing a culturally intelligent consultancy depends heavily on enhancing the skills, attitudes and behaviours of all client-facing staff, and involves the following steps:

- Know your own culture. The starting point for developing cultural intelligence is to establish an understanding of your own firm's culture. Smaller firms are likely to have a single culture because they probably comprise like-minded people and often work within a single sector. The larger consultancies will tend to have a mix because they work across all sectors and have a diverse range of people working within them. Whatever the outcome, the results will allow you to understand what your culture is and how it needs to be adjusted when working with your clients.
- Develop an understanding of your existing clients' cultures. This can be achieved by having your account managers and consultants complete the culture questionnaire or, where appropriate, having your clients do it.
- Embed the cultural intelligence philosophy into your core processes.
- Capture critical information about how you succeed within each of the client cultures, in terms of sales and engagements.
- Capture the hearts and minds of your consulting staff as soon as they join the firm through appropriate induction training and short-term mentoring and coaching.
- Train and educate your existing staff in the application of cultural intelligence.
- Continue the education process throughout the careers of your professional staff. As consultants move up the hierarchy and become less involved with delivery and more with sales and account management, further training will be necessary to ensure the client's culture is taken into consideration when performing these roles. This education should also include an international dimension for those staff who are expected to work overseas.
- Monitor how well you are developing/maintaining your cultural intelligence by introducing a simple measurement scorecard.

The following paragraphs look at some of these steps in more detail.

Cultural intelligence starts at recruitment and induction

From a recruitment perspective, the predictor of successful hiring is based upon the fit of the candidate with the firm's culture. However, what is often overlooked is the individual's own interpretation of how they work within different organizational and national cultures.

The war for talent within all consultancies grows ever fiercer. Having a team of rounded, culturally intelligent and smart consultants should be the objective of every firm. But how realistic is this? After all, the resource pool from which these people can be sourced is limited. Of the consultants you have on your books some will be unable to adjust to the ideals expressed here. For example, I know many consultants who refuse to work in certain sectors. This reluctance occurs for a number of reasons, including previous bad experiences or their having worked in only one sector or having heard bad things about it. This limits their potential and reduces the personal value they can add to clients, their own intellectual capital and the expertise of the firm. Others, who are really able, find it difficult to adapt and instead of changing tend to act in the way they are used to. Unfortunately when an engagement goes wrong they tend to believe that it was because they were not true to form, and next time they try even harder to deliver the assignment in the way they have been used to. In many cases this results in an even bigger failure. If consultancies are to become more acceptable to their increasingly sophisticated clients, they must take steps to recruit the right kind of consultant, and update the skills, knowledge and attitudes of their existing professional staff. So many consultancies have too many of what David Maister terms coasters (those that rest on their laurels) and too few dynamos (those that continually develop themselves and the firm). This has to change.

Consulting firms, and especially those that pride themselves on recruiting the best that industry and academia can offer, take the selection process very seriously. Prospective employees spend weeks and sometimes months in the process. The protracted nature of the process recognizes the need to get a feel for the candidate and assess whether they can fit into the culture of the firm (if only they knew what it was), and investigate their skills. This requires the interviewee to be seen by at least two or perhaps three or more senior members of the firm. The process often involves technical discussions, psychometric testing, assessment centres and role-playing. Collectively these are designed to provide the firm with an overall indication of the candidate's suitability. And, recalling the mix of skills a consultant is expected to have, such assessments predominantly play to the IQ dimension of the candidate's potential. They often fail to capture the emotional resilience and client-handling skills that separate the good consultant from the mediocre. These skills only emerge once the newly recruited consultant is put on a tough assignment. Existing recruitment processes also fail to consider the cultural elements of the work. Clearly if a firm is to become more culturally intelligent it will need to enhance its recruitment processes to assess the degree of cultural sensitivity of its prospective employees. Adding such questions as those listed below will allow the interviewer to gain an insight into the candidate's cultural sensitivity and hence adaptability:

- classify the major differences between, say, an investment bank and an insurance company
- describe the types of changes we might need to make in the way we sell and deliver to these types of client
- describe how you would go about making such adjustments at a personal level
- how would you make these changes in an engagement team you were leading?
- how important do you think culture is to an organization?
- how do you feel about working across different sectors?
- how do you feel about working internationally and within multinational teams?

We also need to recognize the impact national culture has on individuals. As we saw in Chapter 2, nationality defines lifestyle, behaviours, values and attitudes. These may affect the nature of people's perceptions, relationships, activities and ways of communicating. Cross-cultural collaboration can be effective only when all parties understand other cultures. Therefore, other indicators of a culturally intelligent candidate would include the amount of cross-sector experience they have had, the amount of international exposure they have had and how often they have worked within multicultural teams. In general, the more cross-sector and international experience the candidate has, the more likely it is that they will have the requisite skills to adjust to each client. Be warned, however: there are plenty of candidates who will have had overseas experience who have relied purely on their technical skills to get by. So watch out for the obvious stereotyping and arrogance coming out. You should be looking for evidence of adjustment rather than dominance.

With many people entering consultancy after a long spell in industry, testing for cultural intelligence can be a lot harder. Without much cross-sector experience or working experience beyond one or two companies these candidates will tend to have a very narrow view of its importance. However, those who have worked within multinational organizations are likely to have been exposed to different national cultures and hence ought to have some sensitivity. During the interview it would be useful to augment the questions above with others relating to cross-functional change in the organizations they have worked for. Of the candidates that you will interview it is these that will find the transition into consulting and demands of adjusting to different client cultures the most difficult. Training both during induction and once they are in the office is therefore absolutely critical during the early stages of their consulting career.

Induction programmes are necessary tools for all companies. They serve to introduce new joiners into the firm by describing what it is all about, how it is structured, what its basic procedures are and what to expect on day one. This is designed to get the consultants up to speed as quickly as possible before sending them out to clients. But once outside the training room it is pretty much a sink-or-swim environment where the new consultants are expected to fend for themselves. This is bad news because not only does it fail to prepare the consultants for the type of work they will undertake, it also fails to describe how the firm they have just joined works with its clients. If consultancies really wish to develop the cultural sensitivities of their staff they must begin at the induction programme.

I would expect the induction programme to spend at least a half if not a full day discussing how the consultancy works with its clients. This should focus on combining the basic processes (at this stage the delivery of engagements and sales) with client culture to illustrate to the new joiners what to expect. Taking them through a sales and engagement scenario within each of the four cultures would be ideal. This of course would have to be preceded by a short session that introduces the culture model. The use of actors can be a fun and informative way to demonstrate just how different clients can be. The induction should be followed up with further training in the key processes used within the firm and by allocating a mentor or coach. The role of this person would be to reinforce the customer-intimate message and guide the new joiner through the cultural variations they should expect from their clients.

Processes, techniques and tools

Throughout the book I have emphasized the need to update the basic consultancy processes, techniques and tools to meet the needs of the client. It should be stressed that processes techniques and tools are not a panacea for all situations and all contexts. Applying them successfully is down to their use by the consultant(s), and it is here where the culturally intelligent consultant can ensure they are applied in a way that suits the client's culture. The following rules of thumb apply in each of the four cultures:

- Within mercenary cultures processes and tools should be invisible because getting the job done is more important. The overt application of detailed processes and expecting client staff to use them is unrealistic and will not win many friends. If process is to be used it should be cut down to the bare bones and be focused on outcomes. The same applies to the use of tools. Demonstrating that processes and tools can add value both rapidly and with the minimum of fuss is essential if they are to be used by the client. In the end, expediency counts, so it's a case of using an invisible hand rather than ramming process down the client's throat.
- Within networked cultures processes, techniques and tools can be used overtly. Following them religiously is important because it displays repeatability and expertise. It doesn't

really matter if you are using the client's process or your own firm's as long as you're using something. Clients often see the use of processes, techniques and tools as one of the primary means of knowledge transfer between the consultants and themselves, so use it

- Within fragmented cultures the use of process, techniques and tools will be mixed, and this reflects the nature of the culture. Whereas some parts will value the use of these, others will not. Typically the only way to assess this is to ask questions or rely on observation. In the main, the use of processes, techniques and tools can be an effective way to maintain consistency, especially if you will be working across more than one function. The skill in this case will be to make their usage visible in some quarters and invisible in others.
- Communal cultures tend to like the use of processes, techniques and tools, but only if they can see it is adding value. So here it is important to consider what aspects fit the needs of the organization. Therefore stripping the process, technique or tool to its value-adding components is essential.

The best way to approach this variation is to assess your processes, techniques and tools by each culture and make the basic adjustments before you start work with the client. This can be achieved by projecting your standard processes, techniques and tools onto the basic cultural traits of the four cultures and ask yourself the following questions:

- Will this work in its current form in the selected culture?
- What needs to change to make it fit?
- Can the updated process, technique or tool still deliver the results expected of it?
- If necessary, how can we use the process, technique or tool less obtrusively?

This should give you the knowledge of how the process, technique or tool should be applied within each of the four cultures. This information should be captured and then used to brief the engagement team prior to commencing work.

Training

Although some consultants can develop cultural intelligence intuitively, it is unlikely that all will do so. Training client-facing staff ensures that the skills of cultural intelligence are widespread, consistently applied and universally understood. Training should be of two types. The first should aim to introduce staff to the core aspects of cultural intelligence by addressing:

- international cultures, working in multicultural teams and working with the firm's overseas clients
- organizational culture, its impact and importance, and what it means for the firm and the way it interacts with its clients.

The second should address the specific process and inter/intrapersonal training, and cover:

- how the firm's core processes are applied within each of the four cultures
- how emotional intelligence and NLP can help the consultant deal with the variations in working style, politics and conflict within each of the four cultures
- the team and interpersonal dynamics associated with working in the four cultures
- how processes, techniques and tools are used in each of the four cultures.

Creating a database of clients and their cultures

As the firm increases its level of cultural intelligence it will want to capture critical informa-tion about its clients and their culture. Rather than have consultants store this information mentally, and hence failing to make it explicit, it is recommended that a client database is established. This should include information about basic culture, any variations that exist across different functions and, where relevant, geographic regions. In addition, information about specific engagements should be captured and ought to include data on successful and unsuccessful outcomes in terms of client relationships, delivery and lessons that can be drawn out. Once populated this source of information can be used to:

* brief new account managers before they take up their new role
* provide intelligence for all sales pitches in order that they can be crafted to reflect the client culture
* provide the relationship manager with information about the key personalities they will meet and/or be expected to work with
* shape new engagements by highlighting what worked and didn't work in the past
* brief the engagement team as to how they should behave, how processes, tools and tech-niques should be applied, and how the engagement will run.

Measuring success

The culturally intelligent consultancy needs to measure how successful it is in matching its working practices and client-facing behaviours to client culture. A small number of per-formance indicators should be sufficient in this respect, and include:

* the success of sales by culture, measured by the number of wins and losses within each cul-ture
* the number of culture clashes experienced between the firm and its clients, again within each culture; such clashes may be minor (at the consultant level) or very significant (at engagement level)
* the level of cultural intelligence in the firm, measured by the number of consultants trained in the concept, the number of sectors individual consultants have worked within and the amount of international exposure the firm has
* the profitability by each culture.

Targets should be set for each of these and any other measures established. Performance against these can be used to adjust the firm's client-targeting strategy by taking into account its performance in each culture.

Some final advice

ON GOING NATIVE

There is always the risk that consultants will 'go native'. What this actually means in practice is that they lose their ability to remain independent of the client. This manifests itself in the lack of objectivity, jumping to the client's point of view without any consideration of the firm's perspective and failing to raise client issues with the engagement manager. The danger of group think and acting too much like the client can be a very real one, especially if the consultant has been on the same assignment for a period of 18 months or more. This can work against the firm in two ways. For one, if the client values the individual it is highly probable that they will be offered a job. After all if the person concerned has become so like the client's staff it is a great way to secure staff without the overhead of recruitment costs. Second, it may be difficult to complete the engagement because the consultant(s) may be unwilling to rock the boat and hence give difficult messages to the client. I believe that going native becomes an issue where the consultant does not recognize or understand the nature of the client's culture and hence drifts slowly into the client's cultural mould. Therefore being culturally intelligent should prove to be an effective defence against going native because it is predicated on the consultant's taking deliberate steps to understand the client's culture before starting to work with it. It follows therefore that through this understanding the consultant will be more aware of the implications of going native and will be able to recognize the warning signs. The engagement manager must provide a second line of defence, in that they should monitor the behaviours of the engagement team to spot any 'going native' tendencies and deal with them as they arise. In addition there is merit to roll people off an account when they have spent 18 months with the same client. Although this can be difficult because the client may have become dependent upon the consultant, it is a vital action to protect the objectivity of the engagement and the firm.

MAKING THE RESULTS STICK

This is almost the direct opposite of going native. We all know that there are times when the results of the engagement fall by the wayside as soon as the consultants leave the client. This often happens for one of three reasons. First, if the consultants were brought into perform a specific task that is not core to the client's business, once they have completed the job and the problem has been resolved, the client may refocus on their day-to-day business. Second, the client may not value or possess the skills of the consultants. In this case the client feels unable to sustain the results because it lacks the skills and experience, so once again it reverts to its usual activities. Third, there may be an inadequate level of skills and knowledge transfer between the consulting team and the client team. There can be many reasons for this, and it is not always the consultancy's fault. Whatever the reason, the results do not persist. A powerful reason for the lack of persistence may be that the intervention did not take into account the client's culture and hence the way things work within its organization. As a result the desire to embed the change within the client organization can be severely reduced because it is unclear to the client how the change will be of benefit. Adjusting the solution and style of delivery to the client culture will make the results stick far more readily.

ADVICE TO THE CONSULTANT

- Always take time to consider how you come across to your clients – maybe even ask them
- don't think you know best: work with the client not against it
- knowledge exchange is a two-way street – you can learn from the client as much as they can learn from you
- make sure you know how to behave and work in your client's organization – understand its culture
- never assume that a successful engagement in one organization can be replicated in

another without first considering why it was successful in your previous client and what needs to be done to make it successful in the next

- if you are asked to leave a client, consider why: don't assume that it is the client's fault – it may be down to your lack of sensitivity
- when working in multicultural teams, take time to understand what national variations exist in the team and accommodate them.

ADVICE TO THE ENGAGEMENT MANAGER

- Always tailor the engagement structure to the client's culture
- make sure you fully brief the engagement team before it commences work: this should include how to work with the client, what is expected in terms of performance and behaviours, and how the team members will work together
- ensure that the use of processes, techniques and tools is suited to the client: if necessary tailor them first
- keep a watch over the team members for any signs of going native, and where necessary roll them off the engagement
- deal with culture clashes immediately and feed any lessons you learn back into the team and firm.

ADVICE TO THE SALES MANAGER

- Make sure you focus on those things that the client needs you to, not on what you think it does
- if you can speak to the client beforehand and ask where the emphasis needs to be placed, then do so
- take time to sensitize yourself to your client's culture
- remember that you are selling both to the buyer and the culture
- explore with the client how the service should be delivered – does it need a brain surgeon or a pharmacist, for example?
- assess what kind of service and relationship the client wants. Will it be a short-term transaction or a long-term relationship?

ADVICE TO THE ACCOUNT MANAGER

- Always structure the account strategy to exploit the client culture
- determine how relationships are going to be managed and brief the team
- work with the sales and engagement teams to farm the account once established
- if there are major culture clashes discuss this with the client and make any adjustments necessary to eliminate the issue
- use the acculturation model (see Chapter 5) to determine where you want the relationship to go.

Making it happen – Cape Consulting

As a research-based consultancy, Cape Consulting has built up a large body of knowledge about different companies in different industries. Since Cape specializes in helping companies to improve their customer service, and since management style and organizational culture have a significant effect on the quality of customer service a company is able to offer, much of Cape's research for its clients focuses on their culture. Now with many clients behind it, Cape has developed a good understanding of the kinds of culture that prevail in different industries, and prides itself on its ability to implement programmes suited to the particular cultures of particular companies.

Cape Consulting typically works closely with the front line – the most populous group in any service business. This is where Cape is able to rapidly assimilate prevalent cultural characteristics that have an impact on service delivery to customers, for example:

- the degree to which rules are adhered to versus perceived freedom to act
- the nature of communication practices – lateral, top-down, two-way
- what *really* gets talked about at meetings (quotas and volumes, rather than quality and customers)
- who gets noticed, who gets promoted and why, prevalence of company politics.

The consequences of these cultural factors are often felt acutely at the front line and in developing and implementing strategies for service excellence; they must be accommodated before they can be overcome. Cape's constantly accumulating knowledge of business cultures leaves it well placed to cope with the transition from one client to another. Cape has found assessment of the way information flows in a client to be a useful indicator of how Cape can be most effective. For example, in some of the very large clients, customer service excellence can appear devolved between functions. In these cases, Cape has learned to invest heavily and early in discussions to open cross-divisional communication – and sees its own role as bringing divisions together to improve the service experience for customers. When delivering work in this environment, it is very important to make as many friends as possible and to share thoughts openly and regularly. In some of Cape's clients – often in the public sector and in some financial services companies – leadership practices focus on consensus-building. In this environment, Cape has learned to be committed to winning sponsorship beyond the immediate project area and to finding ways of feeding and refreshing enthusiasm, through communications and identifying opportunities for best-practice transfer and joint gains. For those clients that work in fragmented groups, Cape ensures that success is demonstrated very clearly and very early within the engagement. These successes are then used to demonstrate value to others across the client. For others, especially in fast-moving retailers, speed is extremely important, and therefore Cape's responsiveness must be exceptional.

Further reading

Becoming an effective consultant is not a simple process. There are many books that purport to provide the route to success. But success requires the consultant to have a much broader set of skills than many of these books provide. Within this book I have discussed the cultural dimension to selling and delivering valued consultancy. However, this is only part of the wider skill set required. Therefore, in order to provide a comprehensive foundation of the types of skills the consultant needs, I have included a recommended reading list. This covers the range of topics I believe every consultant should be familiar with:

- understanding culture
- understanding yourself
- understanding consultancy
- developing your core knowledge.

Understanding culture

Because an understanding of culture in its widest sense underpins the cultural intelligence concept, consultants would be wise to develop a broad understanding of it. The following books cover the international and organizational dimensions of this essential topic:

- Geert Hofstede (1944) *Cultures and organizations: intercultural cooperation and its importance for survival* (London: HarperCollins Business)
- Rob Goffee and Gareth Jones (1998) *The character of a corporation: how your company's culture can make or break your business* (New York: Harper Business)
- Edgar Schein (1999) *The corporate culture survival guide* (San Francisco: Jossey-Bass)
- John Kotter and James Heskett (1992) *Corporate culture and performance* (New York: Free Press).

Understanding yourself

Self-awareness is increasingly necessary within consultancy. The demands made on consultants continue to grow. Complex engagements, higher expectations, the need to deal with sophisticated and intelligent clients, and assignments that involve working in multicultural teams and across geographical boundaries all demand a more rounded, self-aware consultant. Understanding how to cope with the stresses of consultancy is essential if you are to survive. Therefore it is wise to get to grips with such things as neurolinguistic programming and emotional intelligence. I recommend:

- Joyce Martin (2000) *Profiting from multiple intelligences in the workplace* (Aldershot: Gower)
- Daniel Goleman (1996) *Emotional intelligence* (London: Bloomsbury)
- Daniel Goleman (1998) *Working with emotional intelligence* (London: Bloomsbury)
- Laura Whitworth, Henry Kimsey-House and Phil Sandahl (1998) *Co-active coaching: new skills for coaching people toward success in work and life* (Palo Alto, CA: Davies-Black)
- Jim Steele, Colin Hiles and Martin Coburn (1999) *Breakthrough to peak performance* (London: Catalyst).

Understanding consultancy

Because we all pride ourselves on being consultants – smart, professional problem-solvers – there is a tendency within the community to rest on our laurels. This often manifests itself as arrogance and self-importance, which is why clients hate us – waltzing into their world telling them what to do. It is far better to act with integrity and be more client-centric. Understanding consultancy therefore goes beyond the process-driven models we are used to and shifts our attention to the softer side, which is what makes the difference between the good, the bad and the incompetent consultant. The following books are recommended:

- David Maister (1997) *True professionalism* (New York: Free Press)
- David Maister, Charles Green and Robert Galford (2000) *The trusted advisor* (New York: Free Press)
- Edwin Nevis (1987) *Organizational consulting: a gestalt approach* (London: Gestalt Institute of Cleveland Press)
- Jack Phillips (2000) *The consultant's scorecard* (New York: McGraw-Hill)
- Mick Cope (1999) *The seven C's of consulting* (London: Financial Times Management)
- Robert Shaw (1997) *Trust in the balance* (San Francisco: Jossey-Bass).

Developing your core knowledge

This, as you might expect, is not about developing technical knowledge. Rather it is about some of the additional skills a consultant needs to add value to their clients. For the most part this is associated with handling the subtler aspects of managing the client and delivering the engagement, and resides mainly within the realms of power, politics and knowledge. The only departure from this is the inclusion of project management, which is a core skill many consultants lack. Specific technical knowledge can be picked up through experience, training and reading books. Consultants and consultancies tend to be good at these areas, and in any case they change too quickly to warrant inclusion here. I recommend:

- Dorothy Leeds (2000) *Smart questions: the essential strategy for successful managers* (New York: Berkley)
- Dean McFarlin and Paul Sweeney (2000) *Where egos dare* (London: Kogan Page)
- Gerard Egan (1994) *Working the shadow side: a guide to positive behind-the-scenes management* (San Francisco: Jossey-Bass)
- Thomas Stewart (1997) *Intellectual capital: the new wealth of organizations* (London: Nicholas Brealey)

- Robert Greene (1998) *The 48 laws of power* (London: Profile)
- Jeffrey Pinto and O. P. Kharbanda (1995) *Successful project managers: leading your team to success* (New York: Van Nostrand Reinhold).

Notes

Introduction

1. Biswas, S., and Twitchell, D. (1999) *Management consulting: a complete guide to the industry*, New York: John Wiley, p. 7.
2. Biech, E. (1999) *The business of consulting: the basics and beyond*, San Francisco: Jossey-Bass Pfeiffer, p. 1.
3. Phillips, J. (2000) *The consultant's scorecard*, New York: McGraw-Hill, p. 3.
4. Coles, M. (2000) 'Consultants learn to achieve results', *Sunday Times*, August, pp. 7–14.
5. Abbott, P. (2000) 'Fee income climbs for leading players', *Management Consultancy*, July/August, p. 6.
6. Kemeny, L. (2000) 'HP to pay £14bn for consulting business', *Sunday Times*, 10 September, p. 3.
7. Jones, A., and Bruce, R. (2000) 'Hewlett-Packard ends plan to buy PwC consultancy', *The Times*, 14 September.
8. Kemeny, L. (2000) 'Consultants look to future after "divorce"', *Sunday Times*, 8 October, p. 13.
9. Kemeny, L. (2001) 'KPMG launches its "mission impossible" with £1.3 billion float', *Sunday Times*, 4 February, business section, p. 6.
10. Crozier, C. (2001) 'Outside, looking in', *IT Consultant*, September, pp. 41–44.

Part I: The foundations of cultural intelligence

1. Goffee, R., and Jones, G. (1998) *The character of a corporation: how your company's culture can make or break your business*, New York: Harper Business; Holmes, A., and Jones, G. (1999) *Assessing cultural fit in the sale and delivery of consultancy services*, HWP 9923, Henley Management College, Henley on Thames.

Chapter 1: Where does cultural intelligence fit with emotional intelligence and NLP?

1. Ashford, M. (1998) *Con tricks: the world of management consultancy and how to make it work for you*, London: Simon & Schuster, pp. 263–282.
2. Abbott, P. (2000) 'Fee income climbs for leading players', *Management Consultancy*, July/August, p. 6.
3. Over the last few years there have been a number of books published that help a budding consultant either to enter one of the larger firms, or to establish themselves as an independent consultant. All to a greater or lesser extent touch on the skills required of the

consultant. The following provide some indication of the skills needed: Margerison, C.J. (1995) *Managerial consulting skills: a practical guide*, Aldershot: Gower, p. 8; Nevis, E.C. (1987) *Organizational consulting: a gestalt approach*, London: Gestalt Institute of Cleveland Press, pp. 89–104.

4. There are numerous books covering NLP, and in many respects it has become an industry in its own right, spurring seminars, books, tapes and a variety of self-help texts about how to get what you really want out of life, how to get rich and so on. Although many are selling nothing short of snake oil, there are a few texts that provide a detailed description of NLP that can be extremely helpful to the consultant. I have found the following useful: O'Connor, J., and Seymour, J. (1990) *Introducing neuro-linguistic programming: psychological skills for understanding and influencing people*, London: Thorsons; Laborde, G. (1999) *Influencing with integrity*, Carmarthen: Crown House; Steele, J., Hiles, C., and Coburn, M. (1999) *Breakthrough to peak performance*, London: Catalyst Group.

5. For a useful review of how eye movements can indicate communication preferences, see Laborde, G. (1999) *Influencing with integrity*, Carmarthen: Crown House, pp. 45–74.

6. This case of electorate influence is described in greater detail in Gladwell, M. (2000), *The tipping point: how little things can make a big difference*, London: Little, Brown, pp. 74–77.

7. This model is an extended version of the one found in Harris, C. (1999) *NLP: an introductory guide to the art and science of excellence*, Shaftesbury, Dorset: Element, p. 29.

8. Goleman, D. (1996) *Emotional intelligence: why it can matter more than IQ*, London: Bloomsbury. This was followed up by a book on using emotional intelligence in the workplace: Goleman, D. (1998) *Working with emotional intelligence*, London: Bloomsbury.

9. I would point anyone who is interested in understanding both the research and how the brain functions to two sources. The first is LeDoux, J. (1998) *The emotional brain*, New York: Phoenix. The second is Robertson, I. (1999) *Mind sculpture: your brain's untapped potential*, London: Bantam.

10. The five areas of emotional intelligence are derived from the emotional competence framework in Goleman, D. (1998) *Working with emotional intelligence*, London: Bloomsbury, pp. 26–27, and Goleman, D. (1996) *Emotional intelligence: why it can matter more than IQ*, London: Bloomsbury, pp. 43–44.

11. See Galpin, T., and Herndon, M. (2000) *The complete guide to mergers and acquisitions: process tools to support M&A integration at every level*, San Francisco: Jossey-Bass, p. 171.

Chapter 2: Understanding organizational culture – underpinning cultural intelligence

1. Cartwright, J. (1999) *Cultural transformation: nine factors for improving the soul of your business*, Harlow: Pearson Education, p. 27.

2. Goffee, R., and Jones, G. (1996) 'What holds the modern company together?', *Harvard Business Review*, December, pp. 133–148.

3. Schein, E. (1999) *The corporate culture survival guide*, San Francisco: Jossey-Bass, pp. 15–20.

4. Peters, T. J., and Waterman R. H. (1982) *In search of excellence: lessons from America's best run companies*, New York: Harper and Row.

5. McKenzie, J. (1996) *Paradox: the next strategic dimension: using conflict to re-energize your business*, London: McGraw-Hill, p. 10.

6. Galpin, T., and Herndon, M. (2000) *The complete guide to mergers and acquisitions: process tools to support M&A integration at every level*, San Francisco: Jossey-Bass, p. 171.

7. Stevenson, H., and Cruikshank, J. (1998) *Do lunch or be lunch: the power of predictability in creating your future*, Boston, Massachusetts: Harvard Business School Press, pp. 17–19.

8. The Charles Schwab case came from Pottruck, D., and Pearce, T. (2000) *Clicks and mortar: passion-driven growth in an internet-driven world*, San Francisco: Jossey-Bass, pp. 19–20. The Standard Chartered case came from Saigol, L. (2001) 'Culture clash at StanChart may not be over', *Financial Times*, 30 November , p. 24.

9. Temporal, P., and Alder, H. (1998) *Corporate charisma: how to achieve world-class recognition by maximising your company's image, brands and culture*, London: Judy Piatkus, p. 78.

10. Levitt's 1983 article in the *Harvard Business Review* was 'The globalization of markets'.

11. O'Brien, V. (1996) *The fast forward MBA in business*, New York: John Wiley, p. 217.

12. Jarvis, P. (2001) *Universities and corporate universities: the higher learning industry in global society*, London: Kogan Page, p. 21; Hirst, P., and Thompson, P. (1996) *Globalization in question*, Oxford: Blackwell, p. 18.

13. Langhorne, R. (2001) *The coming of globalization*, Basingstoke: Palgrave, p. 19.

14. Barham, K., and Heimar, C. (1998) *ABB: the dancing giant: creating the globally connected corporation*, London: Financial Times Pitman, p. 151.

15. Downs, A. (1995) *Corporate executions*, New York: AMACOM, p. 11.

16. Ibid., p. 12.

17. Deal, T., and Kennedy, A. (1999) *The new corporate cultures: revitalizing the workplace after downsizing, mergers and reengineering*, London: Orion Business.

18. Reilly, P. (2001) *Flexibility at work: balancing the interests of employer and employee*, Aldershot: Gower, p. 78.

19. Cooper, C. (2000) 'In for the count', *People Management*, 12 October, pp. 28–34.

20. Reilly, P. (2001) *Flexibility at work: balancing the interests of employer and employee*, Aldershot: Gower, p. 25.

21. Galpin, T., and Herndon, M. (2000) *The complete guide to mergers and acquisitions: process tools to support M&A integration at every level*, San Francisco: Jossey-Bass, p. 4.

22. Ibid., p. 2, and Eglin, R. (2001) 'What to do when two worlds collide', *Sunday Times* 17 March, Appointments Section, p. 16.

23. Gordon, J. (2001) 'The end of coziness', *Forbes Global*, 19 March, pp. 44–45.

24. These two examples are taken from: Galpin, T., and Herndon, M. (2000) *The complete guide to mergers and acquisitions: process tools to support M&A integration at every level*, San Francisco: Jossey-Bass, p. 20.

25. O'Shea, J., and Madigan, C. (1999), *Dangerous company: the consulting powerhouses and the businesses they save and ruin*, London: Nicholas Brealey, p. 16.

26. Hofstede, G. (1994), *Cultures and organizations: intercultural cooperation and its importance for survival*, London: HarperCollinsBusiness.

27. Ibid., p. 28.

28. Ibid., p. 51.

29. Andresky Fraser, J. (2001) *White-collar sweatshop: the deterioration of work and its rewards in corporate America*, New York: W.W. Norton, pp. 3–74.

30. Ledger, W. (2001) 'Morale hits all-time low', *Evening Standard*, 13 March, p. 42.

31. Hofstede, G. (1994) *Cultures and organizations: intercultural cooperation and its importance for survival*, London: HarperCollinsBusiness, pp. 82–83.

32. Williams, M. (2001) *The 10 lenses: your guide to living and working in a multicultural world*, Virginia: Capital.
33. Daniel, C. (2001) 'When national stereotypes hold the key', *Financial Times*, 27 November, p. 29.
34. Brown, A. (1995) *Organisational culture*, London: Pitman, pp. 26–27.
35. Machiavelli, M. (1977) *The prince*, W. W. Norton.
36. Wind, J. Y., and Main, J. (1998) *Driving change: how the best companies are preparing for the 21st century*, London: Kogan Page, p. 158. For details on how to deal with the impacts of information politics see Holmes, A. (2001). *Failsafe IS project delivery*, Aldershot: Gower, pp. 131–148.

Chapter 3: Introducing the cultural intelligence model

1. Maister, D., Green, C., and Galford, R. (2000) *The trusted advisor*, New York: Free Press, p. 36.
2. A full description of Westpac's CS90 project can be found in Kennedy, S. (1992) 'What went wrong with CS90?', *MIS*, May pp. 17–24.
3. Holmes, A. (2001). *Failsafe IS project delivery*, Aldershot: Gower, pp. 129–130.
4. Jones, G. (1998) 'Cultural evolution', *People Management*, 29 October, p. 40.
5. Ibid., p. 40.
6. Cohen, D. (2001) *Fear, greed and panic: the psychology of the stock market*, Chichester: John Wiley, p. 206.
7. Jones, G. (1998) 'Cultural evolution', *People Management*, 29 October, p. 44.
8. Lewis, M. (2002) *Sin to win: seven deadly steps to success*, Oxford: Capstone, p. 10.
9. Michaels, E., Handfield-Jones, H., and Axelrod, B. (2001) *The war for talent*, Boston, Massachusetts: Harvard Business School Press, p. 51.
10. Overell, S. (2001) 'All present and correct in the comfort zone', *Financial Times*, 30 November, p. 15.
11. Quoted in Shaw, B. (1997) *Trust in the balance*, San Francisco: Jossey-Bass, p. 116.
12. Gladwell, M. (2000) *The tipping point: how little things can make a big difference*. London: Little, Brown, p. 184.
13. Lowenstein, R. (2001) *When genius failed: the rise and fall of long-term capital management*, London: Fourth Estate, p. 223.

Chapter 4: Cultural intelligence and the consultancy process

1. Lambert, T. (1998) *High value consulting: Managing and maximising external and internal consultants for massive added value*, London: Nicholas Brealey, p. xi.

Chapter 5: Account management

1. Berry, J. (1983) 'Acculturation: a comparative analysis of alternative forms', in Samuda, R. J., and Woods, S. L. (eds) *Perspectives in immigrant and minority education*, University Press of America, quoted in Garrison, T. (1998) *International business culture*, 2nd edn, Huntington: ELM.

2. O'Shea, J., and Madigan, C. (1999) *Dangerous company: the consulting powerhouses and the businesses they save and ruin*, London: Nicholas Brealey.

3. Terazono, E. (1999) 'Look to yourself to get on the right track', *FT Director*, 10 December, p. 11.

4. Collison C., and Parcell, G. (2001) *Learning to fly: practical lessons from one of the world's leading knowledge companies*, Oxford: Capstone, pp. 76–85.

Chapter 6: Sales and sales management

1. Maister, D., Green, C., and Galford, R. (2000) *The trusted advisor*, New York: Free Press, p. 167.

2. Pritchard, J. (1986) *The Penguin guide to the law*, 2nd edn, London: Guild.

3. Walker, K., Ferguson, C., and Denvir, P. (1998) *Creating new clients: marketing and selling professional services,* London: Continuum, p. ix.

4. For some general texts on the link between NLP and selling, see: Brooks, M. (1989) *Instant rapport*, New York: Warner; O'Connor, J., and Seymour, J. (1990) *Introducing neuro-linguistic programming: psychological skills for understanding and influencing people,* London: Thorsons; and Laborde, G. (1999) *Influencing with integrity: management skills for communication and negotiation,* Carmarthen: Crown House.

5. Rackham, N., and De Vincentis, J. (1999) *Rethinking the sales force: redefining selling to create and capture customer value,* New York: McGraw-Hill, pp. 68–69. See also Rackham, N. (1995).

6. Rackham, N., *SPIN®-selling*, Aldershot: Gower.

7. Rackham, N., and De Vincentis, J. (1999) *Rethinking the sales force: redefining selling to create and capture customer value,* New York: McGraw-Hill, pp. 70–95.

8. Maister, D. (1997) *True professionalism: the courage to care about your people, your clients, and your career,* New York: Free Press, pp. 115–118.

Chapter 7: Engagements and engagement management

1. Lambert, T. (1998) *High value consulting: managing and maximising external and internal consultants for massive added value,* London: Nicholas Brealey, p. xi.

2. Egan, G. (1994) *Working the shadow side: a guide to positive behind-the-scenes management,* San Francisco: Jossey-Bass, p. 196.

3. Greene, R. (1998) *The 48 laws of power,* London: Profile.

4. Egan, G. (1994) *Working the shadow side: a guide to positive behind-the-scenes management,* San Francisco: Jossey-Bass, pp. 197–211.

5. Simmons, A. (1998) *Territorial games: understanding & ending turf wars at work,* New York: AMACOM.

6. This section has been brought together from my previous book that addressed the issues associated with software project failure. For more detail on escalation, its origins and what can be done to address it, see Holmes, A. (2001) *Failsafe IS project delivery,* Aldershot: Gower, pp. 59–69 and 149–165.

7. O'Shea, J., and Madigan, C. (1999), *Dangerous company: the consulting powerhouses and the businesses they save and ruin,* London: Nicholas Brealey, p. 29.

8. Ibid., p. 73.
9. *Global IT Consulting Report* (1999) 'IT consultants burning goodwill', November, p. 1.
10. Drummond, H. (1994) 'Escalation in organisational decision making: a case of recruiting an incompetent employee', *Journal of Behavioural Decision Making*, 7, pp. 43–55.

Chapter 8: Relationship management

1. Maister, D., Green, C., and Galford, R. (2000) *The trusted advisor*, New York: Free Press, pp. 22–23.
2. O'Brian, T. C. (2001) *Trust: releasing the energy to succeed*, Chichester: John Wiley, p. 21.
3. Fukuyama, F. (1995) *Trust: the social virtues and the creation of prosperity*, London: Penguin, p. 26.
4. This figure is based on the three foundations of trust described in Shaw, B. (1997) *Trust in the balance*, San Francisco: Jossey-Bass.
5. Maister, D., Green, C., and Galford, R. (2000) *The trusted advisor*, New York: Free Press, pp. 69–84.
6. Figure 8.2 has been adapted from Cleland's model of stakeholder management within projects. For a description of this model, see Cleland, D. (1988) 'Project stakeholder management', in Cleland, D., and King, W. (eds), *Project management handbook*, 2nd edn, New York: Van Nostrand Reinhold, pp. 275–301.
7. Fukuyama, F. (1995) *Trust: the social virtues and the creation of prosperity*, London: Penguin, pp. 23–32.
8. Mole, J. (1999) *Mind your manners: managing business cultures in Europe*, London: Nicholas Brealey, pp. 190–191.
9. Handy, C. (1994) *The empty raincoat: making sense of the future*, London: Hutchinson, p. 80.
10. Greene, R. (1998) *The 48 laws of power*, London: Profile.

Chapter 9: Cultural intelligence and competitive advantage

1. Treacy, M., and Wiersema, F. (1995) *The discipline of market leaders*, London: HarperCollins, p. xi.
2. Maister, D. (1997) *True professionalism: the courage to care about your people, your clients, and your career*, New York: Free Press, p. 103.

Index

For Product Safety Concerns and Information please contact our EU
representative GPSR@taylorandfrancis.com Taylor & Francis Verlag GmbH,
Kaufingerstraße 24, 80331 München, Germany

Printed and bound by CPI Group (UK) Ltd, Croydon, CR0 4YY
01/05/2025
01858344-0001